LIFE THROUGH MY LENS

LIFE THROUGH MY LENS

A MEMOIR

TIMOTHY WHITE

Storyteller
PUBLISHING

Designed in Spain by Francisca Benítez B.

The typefaces used throughout are Tiempos Headline and Tiempos Text, designed by Kris Sowersby for Klim Type Foundry.

Publisher and wholesale inquiries: Storyteller Media,
www.storyteller.media

Cover design by Mohamed Samah

ISBN 978-1-969905-01-8

Edited by Charles Allen

Publisher and wholesale enquiries:
www.storyteller.media

Distributed by macmillan

Printed in CANADA

First Edition: 2026

This memoir is a companion piece to my monograph, *Life Through My Lens.*

For my parents,

and for everyone who shared a moment in front of my lens.

Contents

Foreword

By Julian Lennon

The first time I met Timothy was in 1986. I think Timothy was around 30 years old, and I was just a young, innocent pup...He was there to shoot some publicity shots for my first album *Valotte* and we got on like a house on fire. He was a bit cheeky and arrogant, and a good-looking guy, who was an upcoming photographer from the New York/New Jersey area, and I was a young, shy, but slightly cheeky whippet from Liverpool, so I guess there was something in common there, from the get-go, with our sarcasm and wit in our back pockets. I liked his work so much that I asked him to shoot my second album cover, *The Secret Value of Daydreaming*, which I already had a concept for. I just knew Timothy would be able to bring it to fruition, which he did, and it's still my favourite cover to this day. From this shoot and many others we did together, our friendship grew, because we were very like-minded in many areas, and liked the same aesthetics in photography, design, food, etc....and the list goes on. He's one of those friends who you don't necessarily stay in contact with all the time, but you always check in with, just for a catch up, or to talk about work projects, or to just talk about life...I owe Timothy a lot, for leaning on me to try photography out as a creative medium. Through his guidance and help through my first exhibition called *Timeless* at The Morrison Hotel Gallery in the famous old CBGBs on Bowery in New York City, I found a new drive, a new passion, and a different kind of love for the world. That was a changing point in my life, showing me there were other creative outlets, aside from music, and he obviously had the foresight to see that in me...I've always been in awe of his professionalism, and clientele. It's truly amazing how he's framed Hollywood film and music history through his photographs, being able to capture the essence of each talented artist he's been lucky enough to work with, many of whom have turned out to be the greatest of friends, like Whoopi Goldberg, Billy Bob Thornton, and Harrison Ford, just to name a few...

Though our paths in photography are quite different, had Timothy not pushed me, I would not be the man I am today. He showed me the way, which I followed, and then found my own path...He's a one-of-a-kind friend, who always has your back, and is a visionary man, who's already left an indelible mark in the photography world, as well as in the lives of most the people he meets. Congratulations on this book, Timothy. Finally, the world will be able to know you a little better and be able to hear about all the amazing experiences you've had in your life, that until now, only a few close friends have been privy to before...Wishing you nothing but success.

Julian x

Author's Note

> *"Remember that sometimes not getting what you want is a wonderful stroke of luck."*
>
> \- The Dalai Lama

If people take one look at my life, they assume I get everything I want: The celebrity photography career, creating images for some of the most iconic advertising campaigns, magazine covers, album jackets, and movie posters, luxury travel to the world's sexiest cities, and VIP access to the biggest stars on the planet in the most unique scenarios. What started as a gig taking photographs for the covers of *Vogue*, *Rolling Stone*, or *Vanity Fair* turned into decades-long relationships with some of the legends of entertainment – riding motorcycles across the desert with Brad Pitt, flying airplanes across the country with Harrison Ford, Forging a deep, loving friendship with Whoopi Goldberg – chasing my whims and fascinations with equal obsession. I even bought a town in the Mojave Desert. Just because it seemed like a fun thing to do. *Who does that?* The rewards, the accolades, the success, the lifestyle. The fact that I visually chronicled pop culture history over the last 40 years. When I enter a photoshoot, other people read me as confident and in control. This reputation, which I've had since I told my mom on our way to the first day of kindergarten, "I got this," often precedes me.

Once, someone even once asked me outright, "Tim, do you always get what you want?"

The truth is, I don't—*should I? Does anyone? Is that even the point?*

For years, I used the camera as a vessel to see deeply into the eyes of humanity – every kind of person has been in front of my lens – and yet I've never turned that same lens on myself. Instead, I deflected it on some of the shiniest objects in film, television and music.

I'm often pained for reasons I cannot fully understand. There's more to life, and I am lucky enough to have the ability to search out my truth. I'm looking for answers. What does my soul need? I've been fortunate enough to examine the ups and downs of my life and learn from them. This book is my attempt to put these lessons into context. While I'm proud of all I've accomplished, and expect to be even more so in the future, I've grown to want different things. They're not always tangible. The lens means something much different to me these days. *Life Through My Lens* is a memoir about my life through this evolving lens. For the first time, I'm shedding my persona and pointing a light toward myself.

During my career as a celebrity photographer, I've created a unique series of connections and adventures, and for many years, I traveled the world for photoshoots on a weekly basis, from Russia to Africa to Iceland to bi-monthly trips between California and New York, to the point where I felt more at home in airports and hotels. The smell of jet fuel was exhilarating for me. It wasn't about the money. It wasn't about the celebrity. It was about life experiences and seeing and feeling all of these moments.

Life Through My Lens invites readers into my long-term friendships and relationships – in front of the camera and behind the scenes. The ups and downs from my career, of course, but also of my family and romantic relationships that shaped me, including my early long-term romance with a well-known makeup artist, and later my over 20-year marriage that ended abruptly with a strange, twisted betrayal.

Today, I'm still that guy doing what I love to do. My work and life continue into the present. While I'm more introspective than I've ever been, I'm still doing photoshoots with so much joy and energy and quenchless curiosity. If you were standing by me on a shoot, you'd see me jumping around, laying on the ground, moving everywhere, hungry to get the right shot. I may have more perspective than that 20-something riding his motorcycle around New York City, but he's still just as vibrant as he ever was. I've adapted and been at the forefront of photography in every decade of my career, all while exploring and enjoying a newfound sense of inner stillness I never thought possible years ago.

For these and other reasons, *Life Through My Lens* is for readers looking to find peace in some of the most difficult moments in their lives. As I sit at my desk writing, a framed photo of my father sparkles in the afternoon light. The light always changes. It's never the same twice, even on a photo of my father that stays in the same place on my desk at all times. Under my keyboard, I keep a small, crumpled piece of paper that reads, "This time could be the last time." These are both constant reminders for me to live in the present moment and honor the ones that have come and gone, and those still yet to come.

Chapter 1
The Day I Almost Killed Brad Pitt

Oh fuck. I just killed Brad Pitt.

I slowly pulled over to the side of the road but couldn't park because you can't leave a hot 500-pound motorcycle in dirt and sand. You risk the machine falling and crushing you. I took control of my brain and slowly came to a stop on the side of the road where there was a solid piece of pavement.

The year was 2005, and I was at the top of my game, living the life of a celebrity photographer at the highest level, shooting advertising campaigns for feature films. The highs never got old because I viewed every shoot as an opportunity to challenge myself in new, exciting ways. I was known for being technically proficient, in addition to possessing a finesse for navigating the politics of a movie set – stars, producers, directors, union technicians, etc. – and I'd worked my ass off to become the trusted go-to guy for the advertising agencies involved, to be an on-the-fly psychologist to get the stars to do what I needed them to do, and come back with images that were uniquely my own while trying to creatively please everyone – including myself. I worked hard for years in a fast-paced career to get to this moment where I was one of a handful of photographers with the reputation and trust to do this type of work – and the pay was reflecting my accomplishments. Not an easy job, and one that was earned through years of building trust with not only the client, but also the machine behind the client.

This trust was about to be stretched to the limit. You know how they say, in Hollywood, "You're only as good as your last movie"? For a celebrity photographer, you're only as good as your last shoot.

Enter superstar Brad Pitt.

Here was someone who was also at the top of his game: a two-time *People Magazine*'s Sexiest Man Alive in 1995 and 2000, the star of countless blockbuster movies, and the other half of Hollywood's hottest, most beloved couple. Jennifer Aniston and Brad were the darlings of the moment. Yet, Brad taking on *Mr. and Mrs. Smith* would become a new chapter in the actor's life both personally and professionally – and for me as well.

At the time, I'd been doing some of the biggest movie ad campaigns for the past few years. I got this call to shoot Angelina Jolie and Brad for the movie poster of *Mr. & Mrs. Smith*. I had worked with Angie a couple of times before, but never with Brad. He was the hottest star of the moment. Every woman wanted him, and every man wanted to be him. He was cool, sexy, and I found out that he was really a nice guy. He also liked motorcycles, just like me. I always look for something to talk with my actors about that we may have in common. I know a little bit about everything, or at least I pretend to. My ability to communicate and get people to connect with me has become my stock in trade.

I had a really good friend in New York City named Indian Larry. He was an amazing artist who built custom motorcycles. He built mine. He was kind of a genius and a freak, a sweetheart of a guy, but he looked like a mass murderer. Tattooed all over, including a poem on his neck, he was a guru in the hardcore custom motorcycle world and, more importantly, he was my friend. He died doing a stunt where he rode his motorcycle standing on the seat with his arms outstretched. He called it the crucifix. Sounds insane...well it was. Yet he did it with ease, because he lived his life on the edge, but with a comical sense of humor and a loving heart. Everyone respected him. I was with him on that last ride and was deeply affected by his death. I decided to honor his life with a photobook of eclectic images that I had taken of him and his machines over the 20 years of our friendship.

The book had just come out a few months before this shoot with Brad and Angelina. Aside from my work schedule, I had been tirelessly promoting the now successful publication with interviews and press promotion because it meant so much to me. I'm a Hollywood glamour/portrait photographer, yet this book showed a different side of me and my work. So, when I showed up for this photoshoot with Angelina and Brad, I was excited about life and proud of my work, basking in the feelings of success and the emotions of where I had come from and the directions my career and life were going. It all felt so meaningful.

I had an array of assistants working on pre-lighting the set the day before the shoot. We were prepared and excited about what was going to be a sexy and dynamic photo session with two of the hottest people in Hollywood.

After the initial greetings and introductions, Brad immediately asked me about my book on Indian Larry, and the two of us dove into a focused and lengthy discussion on everything motorcycles and the legendary mechanic. In particular, Brad wanted to know everything about Larry. It seemed we both liked a certain style of dangerous "choppers," bikes that had been stripped down to powerful, two-wheeled hotrods. I couldn't help being a bit perplexed at how my excitement and anticipation of meeting and working with this huge star had taken a turn. My anxiety about being with Brad on an important photoshoot had transformed itself into a different focus —our mutual love of motorcycles and everything Indian Larry. After an hour of this back and forth, which not only excited me because of my bonding with Brad in such a unique way but also relaxed me knowing that we had made a connection that would guarantee his cooperation in completing the extensive shoot I now had in front of me.

Finally, Angelina came out of the dressing room in wardrobe and makeup ready to work, only to find these two boys engrossed in a conversation that had nothing to do with the movie or the reason we were there. She made some comment about getting on with the shoot, and Brad quickly got it together so that we could do what we had come here to do.

During the entire shoot—in between me directing both actors to create a movie poster—Brad kept interjecting comments and questions back to our common interest.

"Tell me about the bike Larry built for you," he said. "How did you work together on it? I love the suicide shift. Is it different shifting a tank shift as opposed to a jockey? It's really all gold leaf and no paint?"

"Well, I had two back operations, so we worked on the ergonomics together because it was going to be a hardtail—no shocks," I said. "Then, Paul Cox got involved and built the airbags under the seat to save my back, which were so cool. Otherwise, I let Larry do his thing and design it his way. He decided on the tank shifter and all the chrome and gold bling. He called it *Tim's Rolex*."

At the end of the shoot and after kisses and high fives on a great job, Brad continued the conversation and made an offhand remark, "Ya know, we should ride together sometime."

"Yeah, I'd love that. As I mentioned, Harrison and I fly and ride a lot, and make a job of it, doing pictures for the studio while doing what we want on our own."

Brad seemed to love the idea. I jumped at the opportunity with enthusiasm, but like I've done with other stars I've connected and built relationships with, I suggested that we make the bike ride part of the publicity photos for the movie. I told him, "I know of a perfect ride through the backroads of the Mojave Desert. We could have an amazing experience and get work done at the same time."

The studio was going to need many images of Brad to promote the film in magazines, and what better opportunity than to go on a ride, have my assistants come along, and allow me to take pictures of Brad during this adventure. It was right up my alley, and I knew I *had* to make this happen.

While I had this incredible concept, it was unlikely that the studio would greenlight a photoshoot that went beyond our current, carefully curated photoshoot for the movie poster, especially one where I absconded to the desert with Brad, their irreplaceable megastar.

After an amazing day, we both went back to our lives, but my odd, mystical friend, Indian Larry, had somehow made a connection between Brad and me. Something spiritual had happened.

It wasn't over.

Two weeks after the movie poster photoshoot, Brad called me and said he had five days to do that ride. I wasn't completely surprised—thanks to my spiritual sign from Indian Larry—but I was excited. I quickly went into action, doing what I do best, and started to produce what would become one of the most memorable of many unbelievably unique experiences that I create around my photography.

First, I had to get Sony Pictures on board. My vision was starting to feel a lot like the beginning of one of Brad's other films at the time, *Ocean's Eleven*. I felt like I was describing a heist and how "all of this will go down." I told my marketing director, "I'm going on a motorcycle ride with Brad, and I want the studio to make it an official assignment. That way, we can use all the photos for publicity and they'll foot the bill." I planned on having my assistants follow us in a motor home along the way with my photo equipment and a stylist with many changes of clothes. This would give me the opportunity to create many different looks for the studio to use in promoting the movie.

The studio still needed more convincing. I'd ridden my motorcycle through the Mojave Desert before, but never with Brad Pitt. This would be a boys' motorcycle trip and an incredible photoshoot. We'd ride through the Mojave Preserve I knew so well and make stops in small towns along the way, including my town of Amboy, California. Located east of Ludlow, CA on Route 66 and about 60 miles from Twentynine Palms, the marine base, its biggest landmark was the Amboy Crater, a 75-mile lava flow and extinct volcano that, if you hiked from its base to the top, would take many hours. The town was in the middle of nowhere, but so unbelievably beautiful. You could even hike up into the cinder cone, something people came from all over the world to do.

I knew the expanse of the two-lane blacktop road that would take us through the desert and to each of these towns. The journey from town to town would be cinematic from a photographic standpoint, giving me a chance to capture pictures of Brad amongst the stunning scenery. We'd do this all while riding motorcycles and stopping a lot along the way. As someone who always lived life for the moment, this was going to be an especially good one.

The studio asked me lots of questions about what could happen while we were out in the desert. "What if it rains?" was one of the questions they asked. I assured them I would get the shots they never knew they wanted, and that no matter what, I would come back with great images.

Still, why would they agree to this?

Because I gained their trust, as only I knew how to do.

Because it was the perfect blend of my vision and their desire to get additional, hot pictures of Brad as we've never seen him before to promote the movie, and, naturally, to make money. The studio would profit from the photos, and, of course, they would have to pay me a lot of money to do so.

My confidence in this plan – and what was in it for them – solidified their decision to say, "Yes."

I was going to do this shoot and ride with Brad no matter what, but having the studio's support both financially and otherwise helped to make this happen for us both.

Once we had the greenlight, my team and I prepared for days. My assistants and stylist rented an RV and filled it with racks of clothes. Brad's assistant coordinated getting our motorcycles from LA to the desert in his pick-up. The idea was to drive to Barstow, get out of LA proper, unload the bikes, and once we arrived in the desert, finally start the adventure.

There was one problem I hadn't foreseen: Brad couldn't leave his house without the paparazzi tailing his every move. Gossip rags like *The National Enquirer* were printing salacious headlines about his personal life every day. I was strongly in the corner of "all publicity is good publicity," but it was causing a logistical nightmare when I finally arrived at Brad's house to pick him up for the photoshoot.

I first pulled up on Indian Larry's motorcycle in front of Brad's house in Hollywood that sunny, fall day, followed by our motorhome full of clothes and crew. As I pulled up, Richie had Brad's two bikes already loaded up on the truck. We then loaded up my bike. I walked into the house and said hi to Brad, who was still getting ready. Back outside, I finished tying up the motorcycles on the truck. We weren't exactly a subtle sight. A helicopter circled over his home. I felt as paranoid as Ray Liotta in *Goodfellas*, wondering if we'd already been found out.

We needed to get him away so that we could do this trip unencumbered and alone. The trick was to whisk him out of LA, unnoticed. We'd figure it out, I thought. At least, that's what I hoped.

Then, Brad walked out of his front door and onto the driveway wearing a gray hoodie, t-shirt and jeans, looking like the epitome of cool. Young. Rich. Famous. His assistant walked out next and made sure his pick-up with our bikes was ready to go.

I felt a rush of adrenaline as Brad hopped into the passenger's seat. Our caravan began backing out of the driveway. Getting through the first leg of this journey was crucial. We knew it was important to quietly get him out of town so people wouldn't follow us. This adventure was so in my zone, and yet I had serious anxiety about the possibility of hitting an obstacle that canceled the whole shoot. I needed to control the pessimistic version of the experience that was playing in my head, and make sure the experience came off the way I envisioned it. Back then, this was all about me. I was in my own world.

I kept looking over my shoulder. A car changing lanes made me think twice.

For now, though, it was up to the universe. We were enroute to Barstow, a little less than two hours out of L.A. and in the desert. We pulled into a gas station to fill up and get ready for the last few miles before unloading and getting started. Brad told me he needed the restroom.

"Keep your hoodie on," I said as Brad left the car and walked into the gas station convenience store. I pumped gas as my anxiety crept higher and higher. What would happen if someone recognized him? Would our trip be over before we even got to the desert? Would the press find out? I wanted to be sure nothing interrupted this moment. At this point, outside of the desert location we were headed to, I had no control over my environment.

After refilling the tank, I stepped inside to pay the cashier and looked for Brad. When he came back from the restroom, no one seemed to give a second thought as to who he was.

The hoodie worked. He appeared casual enough to just be a regular guy. That's what I hoped people would think, and thankfully they did. As we all jumped back into the vehicles, a sense of relief overcame me.

We drove deeper into the desert. At our next stop, we unloaded our motorcycles off the pick-up and prepared to hit the road. Who had a better life than me at this moment? I was getting paid to photograph the most famous celebrity of the time while on a motorcycle trip.

We started smirking as we rode, finally at ease and enjoying the ride. The feeling of a machine roaring between our legs without the restraints of a federal law approved, factory manufactured bike—a chopper—made us both feel like cowboys in the wild west. There we were, a newer version of that, something like modern cowboys. Rebels *with* a cause. A shared goal of a photoshoot and a shared love of motorcycles. We began riding toward Amboy, CA, the town I had purchased on a crazy whim, a hundred miles in the middle of the Mojave Preserve. There was nothing out there but desert. This was rough territory. A hundred- and twenty-degree days in the summer were not uncommon. In the 1880s, they built the railroad to cross the desert, and train stops became little stores, which then became towns in the middle of nowhere. The railroad stops were each named alphabetically, Amboy being one of them. In the early 1930's a man named Roy Crowle bought land in Amboy and built a motel, a gas station, a repair shop, a cafe and other buildings that took his name; Roy's Motel and Café and became landmarks for the town. When Route 66 was built in 1926, it became a way to cross the country. During the Great Depression, people packed up their farms and traveled to California looking for a new life. Amboy became a road stop for them and continued to grow through the years.

When I first found this town while on an earlier motorcycle ride, the look and feel of this weathered, desolate place felt as if I stepped into a piece of Hollywood-designed history. There was a sign that said the entire town was for sale, and I bought it. That was 1998, and now, eight years later I was sharing this piece of real-life cinema with Brad. We stopped at the cafe for lunch. Roy's Motel and Cafe was built out of railroad ties in the '40s, while the cabins around it were from the '30s and hotel rooms were built in the '50s. It was layer upon layer of something so raw, so real, so American, that I felt like I was participating in my own version of carrying forth a piece of history.

Over burgers and beer—that's all the cafe had—we talked about my friend Indian Larry. He had been an addict and a convict. He was homeless and a criminal. But then he got sober and became famous through reality television. His unbelievable ability to create the most beautiful and mechanically perfect custom motorcycles made him a legend. He built my bike. In a sense, Indian Larry brought Brad and me together. We shared our mutual love for Indian Larry's motorcycles and how it felt to ride on them. Brad was fascinated by my relationship with this motorcycle shaman and was very into the motorcycle subculture.

After lunch, we jumped back on our bikes and left Amboy. A few miles up, we took a left on Kelbaker Road and headed north. At the top of a pass, I saw a great vista and beautiful light. I needed to pull over and capture something. Our first photo of the ride. I gestured to the Winnebago to stop where we were. As my assistants got out and I directed them to set up the camera and a light, I found myself talking fast and feeling the adrenaline rush of riding the motorcycle, being with Brad, and now feeling the rush of seeing a picture about to happen. I only had so many hours in the day to do as many setups and take as many pictures as I could.

I started snapping photo after photo of Brad leaning over his bike, dressed in faded gray jeans and a black jacket over the gray hoodie he'd hidden in just hours before. His sunglasses were nestled in his hair as he stared out into the desert, looking calmer than I'd seen him back in LA. The mountains behind him were the perfect backdrop. I didn't stop shooting until I felt I had enough photos to work with. Just as suddenly as we had stopped, I was handing my camera back to my assistant, jumping on my bike and we headed out again.

This was our rhythm. Ride, stop, shoot, and move. The ride was exhilarating and relaxing at the same time. Riding a motorcycle is like surfing or flying a plane. There is a focus that's razor sharp, yet you're in a moment unto yourself. You're in your own head, and there's peace. But when I see something and pull over, there is a different kind of adrenaline that takes over. That's when my fast-paced shooting style begins again. A waterfall of words cascades from my mouth as I work in split seconds to get the shot.

I direct the shooting with precision and bask in my element. Along with this command of my moment and my craft, come thoughts that I usually keep inside.

As I shot image after image, there was still an insecurity that told me that this was purely a theatrical experience. A show I was putting on. A play I was acting in. I wrote it. I created it. For a moment between each shot, I wondered why this movie star was interested in doing this with me? Logically I knew this equality in the relationship between me as a photographer and celebrities was something that I nurtured my whole career, even when I didn't believe it. People could see I was relaxed, controlled, and apparently confident, and word-of-mouth spread. It's what built and perpetuated my career. But an artist always has this duality of insecurity and ego. That is the balance that makes us need to express ourselves.

Brad, for the moment, thought I was cool. And I was, whether Brad thought so or not. Ha! I had to remind myself that I was the only person who could get a star like Brad to agree to this kind of shoot. Or did Indian Larry make this happen? My style is unique. Not necessarily the technical side, but definitely my ability to create an experience that is totally me. Sometimes I don't have a plan, a location or an angle, the right light or the right lens. But I always find a perspective. Both literally and figuratively. I can look and say, "This is kind of what I envisioned," and build on that. In my mind I can see something. A background. A landscape. And see my subject in it. There can be an object that inspires me. A rock, a tree, a car...I can see them just standing in the middle of the street or sitting anywhere with their hands in their pockets...whatever it is, it becomes the reason that makes the image I create something special. The convergence of all the pieces brings together a composition that just makes sense in my mind. It's a vision realized. One way or another, it comes together and says something. I make it happen even when I seemingly don't know exactly what I'm doing. That confidence overrides my insecurities. It's all pretty fascinating to me.

The light was beginning to go, and our next stop was 80 miles away. It was a good hour ride or more. While I was ready to make more stops and shoot into the night, we still had to reach the small town where we would sleep for the night. We got to the bottom of this hill and headed into a small town named Kelso, where nobody really lived anymore, but it was still a junction for trains. In this area of the country, most of America's goods were transported across the country via train. These freight trains were sometimes two miles long.

As we approached the railway tracks from a mile away, the red warning lights started flashing and the bars came down. The freight train was blocking our road, and we had to wait for over an hour for it to pass. We grabbed beers out of the cooler and took some photos. I was starting to get anxious because the day was fading fast. When the train finally moved, we passed through as the sun began to set. I didn't see the moon yet and the sky became very dark. We were in one of the most beautiful parts of this stretch of desert. My plan was for us to stop at our motel, eat dinner and take photos into the night. We'd shoot with flashlights, car headlights, any light we had. Anything that would look cool.

We started riding on a road with rough patches, reminded that these custom bikes weren't factory-made motorcycles, nor were they federally inspected and approved. They were one-off, hand-built machines. It was getting darker and darker outside. No moon. No other vehicles. We couldn't see anything in the desert except for the headlights on our motorcycles. As an experienced rider, I was comfortable staying in the middle of the road with Brad to my right. All of a sudden, I saw Brad start to get a front wheel wobble. The geometry of his particular machine may not have been right at that particular speed on that road. When he started to get a wobble, I knew he had to slow down. Otherwise, he could wipe out. I watched in horror as his headlight trailed off the road.

He was gone.

I freaked out.

"Brad! Brad!" I yelled into the pitch-dark night.

Seconds went by that felt like years.

"I'm over here," he finally said.

I raced to Brad's side. He was on the ground and had fallen on his knees, palms, and his forehead. We'd been going 40 miles an hour and thankfully he had the right helmet on, unlike me. He was scraped up, but he was mostly in a bit of shock. He was laying in the road, shivering in the middle of nowhere. I couldn't imagine what he was thinking. My first instinct was to lay over him because he was cold.

"Tim, look," he said.

The Winnebago, which was miles behind us, was now barreling down the road toward us lying in the middle of the road. I waved my arms to catch their attention. My two assistants and Brad's assistant and my stylist leapt out. We got him up, inside of the Winnebago and set him up with an ice pack.

"Brad, the last thing I want to do is stop right now, but you don't fall off of a motorcycle at this speed without getting checked out," I said.

"No, I'm fine," he said.

But I insisted. We were about 80 miles from Vegas and 20 miles from the next little town I had planned as our stop for the night. As much as I didn't want to leave him, he had to go.

"You need to get checked out at the hospital," I insisted.

Brad's bike was also broken, so they loaded it back on the vehicle. I chose to ride alone to the town, and the Winnebago crew would meet me there later. Brad and his assistant went ahead to Vegas. I was deep in my thoughts. Brad was OK, but bruised. This had been my moment. And I had no idea whether I'd get to finish the shoot. I wondered if I would have to come back to the studio with only the photos I took earlier in the day.

Around 8:00 a.m. the next morning, Brad called me.

"All right, I'm good," he said. "Come get me. Let's go."

Fuck yes, I thought, feeling grateful.

"Stay where you are," I said. "I want to shoot pictures of you in your hotel room."

"No, I'll meet you..."

"No wait there for me, I really need to shoot something other than desert landscapes, I want to get some variety."

After he was discharged from the hospital the night before, he ended up in a nice hotel in Vegas. While it was the best hotel in Vegas, it was still just a hotel room at the Ritz, meaning, it wasn't visually unique.

I had to make it special. I do that with light. I do that with a lens. I do that with intent.

We shot against the headboard behind his bed and played with the lighting. He was lying in bed in a white undershirt and underwear. His scraped knuckles from his fall the night before were front and center. He was leaning forward in bed, just a sliver of his hip showing. The right amount of sexy. I took the photo with the right lens, with the right light. I may have gone through 200, 300 frames to get to this now iconic shot.

We wanted to go back to the desert, but Brad's motorcycle was still broken. Luckily, I knew somebody who owned a shop in Vegas. They were real hardcore biker types who built and worked on choppers. I took Brad over there, and his eyes widened with excitement. He loved being in a real bike shop and seeing all of the motorcycles in various states of repair. In turn, these tattooed, hardcore bikers who owned the shop were excited to see Brad. Everyone started talking to each other, laughing and sharing stories. While I loved that everyone was getting along, we had to head back to the desert and not waste anymore daylight.

"OK guys, we gotta go take pictures," I said.

The guys at the shop asked if they could come ride with us. I shrugged. Why not? Brad was into it and so these guys tagged along on our shoot. At this point, I didn't want to take the same kind of pictures in the desert, among Joshua trees, cactus and dust. We already did that. As we turned into yet another gas station, a man in a mud-splattered 1963 Impala swerved in while we were sitting there getting gas. It was a beat-up Chevy with mud all over it. It was just perfectly cool.

When the guy went into the convenience store, I ran after him in my style. I burst into the mini mart and got his attention.

"Hey, can you please leave your car at the pump?" I said. "I'd like to take some photos with it. I'll buy your six-pack of beer."

Puzzled but also flattered, he agreed.

I went back outside and had my stylist change Brad into a sleek charcoal gray suit. As we were now blocking the gas pumps, people started to look at us. *Oh, that's that movie star*, their faces seemed to say. Because we were still technically in the middle of nowhere, they understood who he was, but also didn't quite get it. They watched as I put up a light and he leaned one hand against the car. We were making this photoshoot look fun and easy while there was this surreal scene of Brad and a bunch of bikers hanging around. Brad's smoldering expression as he looked into my camera lens sealed the moment.

While we were getting ready to hit the road again, one of the guys from the bike shop gave me an idea for a unique shooting location.

"What about the Chicken Ranch?" he said. "My old lady works there."

The Chicken Ranch was a legal brothel in Pahrump, Nevada about 60 miles away. I looked over at Brad as if to ask, "Should we go?" He gave me the thumbs up.

We were going.

The biker put me on the phone with the Madam to arrange our visit.

The Chicken Ranch was in the High Desert, a dry, mountainous region dotted with scrub bush in a higher elevation than the Low Desert, where we had been yesterday. As we drove up the winding dirt road and got off our bikes, we saw the brothel was only a series of double-wide trailers connected together with a fake facade, like a movie set. I was in heaven. I'd found my unique location.

I asked Brad to sit in the middle of this dirt road leading up to the house. There was something about him that the camera knew what to do and he knew what to do for the camera. We took the photo right outside of the Chicken Ranch. There was almost no light left in the day. The lens was wide open with a shallow depth of field. The High Desert surroundings were out of focus while Brad was in sharp focus.

Then we walked inside the brothel. Although I'd had many different experiences in my life, I'd never been into a brothel. It was over the top, but not in a good way. Not dirty bad, just bad. Several women, dressed in lingerie, greeted us at the bar, which consisted of cheesy velvet banquettes and cherry wood tables. The women took out their phones and snapped pictures of him. While they talked over beers, I started scouting a shoot location. I'd already shot a photo of him in bed, and taking photos of him in bed at a brothel seemed tacky and too obvious.

I found a tunneled hallway that was wood paneled from floor to ceiling. This worked. It was a vortex. It was the only thing that took me out of the depth of this boring motor home hell. I set up the lighting, testing with Polaroids, and built the photo to make a scene. I approached two women at the bar. There was something about them that was odd, but what *wasn't* odd about this place? I asked if they would pose naked for the photo. They agreed.

Then I had to go find Brad in one of these double-wide trailers. I found him in the kitchen sitting at a table with a few of the sex workers. They were sharing a platter of salmon and salad. Too surreal. I told him I was ready to shoot. He walked into the hallway. We dressed him in a suit with a hat and got him to lean against the wall. The two women stood behind Brad, lost in their own world. They were clinging to each other, naked, as they rested against the wood-paneled tunnel. Brad looked off to the side while they looked into the camera.

The context of Brad and the women being in a brothel disappeared in this location, which was what I was going for. Then we took pictures outside by the neon sign of the Chicken Ranch...just because we had to prove we were there. After thanking everyone for their hospitality at the brothel, we got on our bikes and headed back to Vegas. On the ride back in the dark, I kept thinking about Indian Larry. The whole day and this location were a circus.

Just like Larry's life. He made this happen, I thought. Somehow, he had been with me on this whole journey with Brad.

The trip continued and then led to more opportunities to bond with Brad and have many more photo shoots with him over the years. The connection to Indian Larry that brought this experience together has been a theme throughout my life and career. Each person who has touched or influenced me, continues to do so. There are constant uncanny and mystical connections that are links of a chain that thread through my life. The images that I capture come from natural situations, yet there is something supernatural about each experience. I mostly shoot without a plan. Out of that "without a plan" strategy, I can be fully present in the moment, all the while capturing that moment for history. The way that I live and the work that I do is part of the story of my life and the story of the lives that I touch with my camera. As I photographed Brad and other celebrities over the course of their lives, I created multiple moments and a document of their time. I crafted an image, a story that would carry on forever. What I did was really an accomplishment for the people in front of my camera, but also for me. The moment was mine just as much as it was theirs.

When I got home, my "all press is good press" motto was tested: Brad, the darling of the

National Enquirer, was on the front page again, and this time with his new friend: Yep, me.

The headline screamed off the page: *Brad's Brothel Shocker.* So did the quote, *"All I had on was my shoes when I got naked."* The quote was attributed to "Hooker Brooke," a woman pictured next to the article. Sprawled over a leopard print couch, her shiny high heels dangled off the edge. Her face was blurred out. A small photo of a sign read Chicken Ranch, the whorehouse Brad and I had stopped in while we were riding our motorcycles through the desert for our now infamous photoshoot.

Another two-page spread of Brad riding on his motorcycle in better days accompanied the article, which recounted the details of his accident. The one I had watched with my own eyes. The one that left me second guessing my own decision-making. All of that work as an expert at shooting advertising campaigns for the film industry hung in the balance – or did it?

Would my career survive this kind of scandal?

Ha, of course it would. In fact, it only added to my mystique as a Hollywood photographer who experienced these kinds of things with these stars. It only helped each of our careers.

Years later when I was on the set to shoot the campaign of the Ocean's Eleven sequel, Brad introduced me to George Clooney. George shook my hand and gave me a little smile.

"Oh, so you're the guy who almost killed Brad."

Chapter 2
A Kid from New Jersey

The seeds of my future celebrity photography career were planted early on for me. I was born in 1956 in New Jersey, the youngest of three kids to two parents with polarized personalities. Although they were both born in 1919 and lived through the Great Depression and WWII, my parents couldn't have been more different from each other. My father was a quiet, simple man who worked as a civilian comptroller for the Coastguard while my mom was a demanding, spoiled housewife who wanted more than she had and seemed to blame everyone for everything. She demanded that my father take her to dinner and a show in Manhattan on Saturday evenings. He commuted to work there every day of the week, but he'd drive her from Jersey into New York City even though he would have preferred to stay home and watch golf on TV. My two sisters and I wished he would speak up for himself. We were angry at our mom for seemingly pushing him around in these ways. And yet, my mom's rollercoaster of demands and emotions helped to shape my own personality. It's funny, but it took many years before I could see that I ended up living a more glamorous, jet-set life than my mom could ever dream of, yet had many of the same traits. It took even more time until I saw myself taking on not just some of her personality, but the same deferential role as my father in some of my own relationships.

My mom had anxieties and fears and was too self-involved to give me the attention I needed. I constantly wondered, "What about me?" and began to take on more self-reliant qualities because I didn't feel I had her love and needed to take care of myself. By the time I started kindergarten, I had forged my own sense of independence. I let go of my mother's hand and said, "I got this, Mom," and walked into my first day of school.

My mom was tense and uptight, a stark contrast to her large, boisterous, and often colorful Italian family. Yet, she had a galvanizing effect on all the other family members. You could be furious with her one week and love her the next. They reacted to her with distrust and annoyance. Just when you thought you were out, she pulled you back in with her sudden sweetness and charm. She was a son of a bitch, yet gave herself charitably to people and causes beyond what most people are capable of. She somehow managed to be a very fashionable woman too, despite my father's meager salary. She always seemed to dress hip and of the moment and always looked more together than her means.

My dad was somewhat the opposite. He kind of "MacGyvered" everything, including his wardrobe dress. On weekends he'd pull down a pair of jeans that hung in the garage that he wore for chores. He used an old electric lamp cord as a belt, but in true Joe White fashion, he only tied the cord between the first two loops. I guess that's all you really needed to pull the waist together and hold your pants up. He was quirky and funny, but very down to earth.

When I was a little boy, he knew of my interest in being a fireman. When we heard the nearby sirens from the volunteer fire department, we'd leap from the dinner table and jump into his car to follow the trucks. He was very youthful in his joy for the simplest of things and would always treat me like I mattered. I was his only boy, and there was something about our relationship that we both were always comfortable with.

Mom, on the other hand, made everything about her, and was always angry at something. Consequently, we all walked on eggshells around her not knowing when the next storm would arrive.

My grandmother lived close by in a neighboring town. Her home was a revolving door of relatives who all lived there at times before moving on and buying their own homes, including my parents and various other family members. My grandmother also hosted epic, unforgettable Sunday dinners. My grandfather owned a fish market, so there was always lots of seafood at dinner. For those meals, they cooked the fish in the tomato sauce and made these rich shrimp, scallop and lobster sauces, or as some Italians called them, gravy. These sauces would simmer for eight hours and turn the meat of the fish into something smoother than butter. It melted in your mouth. The meals weren't fancy, just homey Italian cooking. When dinner was ready, the table was set and took up the whole room in the basement kitchen. My young cousins and I would run around while everyone sat and ate. Many of these family gatherings would be immortalized in the snapshots of our family albums, which I now realize were my introduction to photography representing a visual document of family history.

My dad was an only child, and his parents died when he was young. So I grew up without his side of the family and without that other German/Irish cultural influence that his parents would have brought to our family. We heard very little about his parents growing up so we were more involved in my mother's Italian side.

The cast of characters in my mother's family, on the other hand, fed me both emotionally and physically throughout my childhood. Every holiday, family ritual, or special event was spent with someone on the Coppola side. There was Uncle Louie, who dressed like a dandy and swanned into family gatherings once a year from where he lived in Pasadena, California.

We had no idea who he really was or what he did...but he dressed and acted differently and was a relative, nonetheless. His style was certainly different from the rest of the family in Jersey. Uncle Tony – the Captain or Cappy – was associated with gangsters, spent time in prison, and was my mother's version of the family black sheep. He had an independent style and attitude, and everyone treated him as if he had something going on. But in truth, he was a deadbeat. I thought Uncle Tony was the coolest and saw his free lifestyle as something unique. He brought these tough guys to my grandmother's for dinner. They wore pink shirts, silver ties, and pinky rings. I thought they were so different, yet they seemed to fit in with our family. I was too young to really understand who they were, though. Cappy's persona evoked a fascination with the mafia and gangsters for me that's continued throughout my life and career. This continues to always be some association with my interests. Maybe it's Hollywood, maybe the freedom of lifestyle...maybe it's the Cadillacs, but I continually find myself intrigued with the gangster image. Aunt Lucy and her husband Uncle Tony Fasciano taught me many things as a little boy, and I had a close relationship with them. Aunt Lucy wore these funny wigs and had coke bottle glasses. Tony was big and masculine and had enormous hands. They were more old-school Italian, and shared home remedies and a way of living that was from another time and place. There was Uncle Chappy. *These nicknames!* His real name was Louis, but he seemed to walk with a waddle when he was younger and picked up the nickname after Charlie Chaplin. He was a short little man who worked with my grandfather in the fish market and eventually took it over after grandpa's death. His wife Josephine was a large woman who had a tough demeanor and always scared me as a child. Closer to home was my widowed Aunt Phil or Filomena, whose husband died very young and who lived upstairs from my grandmother with her two daughters. Aunt Phil was quite a character, *like they all were,* who did what she had to do to survive, including running a numbers lottery in the neighborhood for Uncle Tony who also lived at home with my grandmother when he was either out of prison or not wandering around with his hoodlum chums. Phil had a way of speaking that was rough and streetwise, yet she was a strong single parent to my cousins Jeannie and Patty. She was also hysterically funny. She drove a school bus for handicapped children. I remember that she used to beep her horn and wave as she drove by me as I was walking home from school with a bus load of kids with cerebral palsy. All my aunts and uncles were strong and unique people who taught me how to survive just by their example.

Throughout my childhood, I began to cultivate my own interests that somehow seemed attached to my family's colorful personalities. I loved watching old black-and-white movies starring Robert Mitchum and Humphrey Bogart, finding myself drawn to the coolness of the characters and style and how wardrobe and lighting was at play in creating the narrative. As a young teenager I used to sit up late at night watching the Late, Late Show until 3:00 in the morning, smoking cigarette butts from the ash tray and holding them in my fingers, pinched in the way I would eventually shoot a photo of Robert Mitchum. Film, in its essence, is just a series of still photos, and I definitely saw something in capturing moments that came from those movies. Although photography as a career wasn't even a thought for me yet, I enjoyed other forms of visual art and embraced what I'd later describe as an alternative way of seeing and living.

By the time high school came around, I was into art, surfing, motorcycles, doing drugs, and immersing myself in the music of the time. Throughout high school and then college, my trajectory toward a career in photography would become clearer and clearer. My alternative hippie era persona of the early 70s, led me to think that a career having something to do with horticulture and the arts would be a path I might take post high school. I worked in nurseries and a florist shop after school and thought combining that interest to design would be cool.

During my senior year, I took one step toward a career in visual arts: My sister Mary's husband, Dennis, a cool guy who wore second-hand outfits and leather coats and was like the big brother I never had, introduced me to the world of landscape architecture. I wasn't totally sure what it was about, but it seemed to fit my interests at the time and some sort of professional adult future.

Concurrently, I was also playing around with cameras, photographing my friends and local bands, and looking at as many music magazines and album covers as I could. I was also getting a sense of the world of photography and how it was being accepted as an art form. I went to museums and galleries and started to feel something about photographic imagery that clicked – *sorry* – with me.

I also knew that I wanted to get away from my small-town New Jersey existence and looked into colleges on the West Coast. California seemed so free, warm and exciting, and the music scene there was in full bloom. Although I did pretty well in school, I didn't have the academic or financial ability to get into any of the West Coast schools that had accredited landscape architecture programs. I looked into the University of Arizona, and it seemed to have all that I was looking for: warm weather, far from Jersey, an accredited landscape architecture program, an almost West Coast distance, something more affordable, and a beautiful environment.

I traded my '68 Volvo for a beat-up '62 Ford pick-up truck from my boss at my summer job. I had already been driving his truck as a florist delivery person during the summer, smoking pot and listening to disco hits like "Rock the Boat" and "Do the Hustle" along my route. The truck was a piece of shit, but had enough room for all of my belongings, including my more than 300 album collection, stereo system with huge speakers, and cheap wall tapestries which were all the rage at that time. My boss definitely got the best of the deal. The floorboards were rotting. Oil leaked so badly from the engine that it flew up into the cab and burned my legs as I drove the long distance across the country. I had to stop constantly and refill it with engine oil. I would pull into fields and sleep under the truck at night since the cab was too short for me. On one occasion, I woke up with cows all around me.

Once I reached Tucson, AZ, I was worlds away from New Jersey and found myself close to the Mexican border. After arriving and being on my own for the first time, I felt the exhilaration of adulthood and independence. While I was always living life on my terms, I was beginning to expand that definition and loved being in a completely new environment. I found an off-campus apartment that was like Melrose Place for college students. We all smoked pot and did Quaaludes and partied around the pool in the 110-degree weather, me in my short shorts, midriff-baring shirt and trendy poodle haircut of the time. The 70's. What a look.

I started my classes and quickly realized that my chosen major required a lot of math, a subject that I had trouble with despite my dad being an accountant. I also came from a very liberal East Coast/NYC background, and Arizona was a bit more conservative than what I was looking for. Plus, it was hot as hell. My disappointment with my choices gave me a reason to explore beyond academics, and I started enjoying the beautiful landscape surrounding Tucson by exploring, motorcycle riding, getting high, and taking pictures. I also discovered a creative photo scene brewing and one gallery in particular, and I started to hang around there and help with exhibitions and absorb as much as I could. This was a rarity since photography was just beginning to be taken seriously in the art world in the early 70s. Unknown to me at the time, but the U of A school president was totally into photography and with his influence the school had just acquired a huge photographic collection and had built a library to house it. But there was no photography department, and I knew I was in the wrong major.

Although classes were not compelling enough for me, my social life was flowing, and the party scene at college was a ramp up from my high school experience. I was free, fun, stoned, and popular. The pool party at my apartment building was insane, and I was right in the middle of it.

Little did I know that, here, I'd meet my future girlfriend and would-be makeup artist icon Bobbi Brown, a relationship that would eventually help to catapult me into the role of celebrity photographer. My friendship with Bobbi would turn into something much more in the coming years, but when I met her at the U of A, she was dating her high school sweetheart, and we all became close friends. Bobbi and I came from very different worlds: She was a rich kid from the comfortable suburbs of Chicago while I was a middle-class kid from Jersey who assimilated easily in social situations and could hang out with all kinds of people in some way or another. So, we spent more and more time together. She had been seeing her boyfriend who was from her hometown since middle school, but it seemed obvious to me that she was having more fun with me than with him. As friends, Bobbi and I continued partying together and forming our bond.

Chapter 3
Breakup

I finally decided after a year that Arizona and landscape architecture wasn't for me. I took a semester off and moved to Boulder, CO where some friends were going to school. I moved into a big house with a bunch of guys, which all seemed pretty much right out of the movie *Animal House*. The house was a mess, we were all pigs, and we threw the best parties anywhere off campus. My life of sex, drugs, and rock and roll had now become a part of my identity. The party only got bigger. When I wasn't partying, I found myself more interested in learning about and taking photographs. I spent the year working, taking pictures, partying, and applying to other colleges. I knew this particular party was not sustainable, and I wanted to immerse myself in art and a college education. I applied to and got into the Rhode Island School of Design for the fall semester and planned my trek back across the country during the summer. It was a big, independent decision for me, and I felt like I was starting a new creative life adventure. Before I had left Arizona, I had gotten a dog. A white shepherd/golden retriever mix I named Jessie. She followed me everywhere, and spent every moment with me. She was not only my best friend, but an amazingly gentle and intelligent animal. She was my partner. In June, we headed across the country in my ugly green VW van to get to Rhode Island in time for a six-week summer session I had to attend before the full semester began in September.

My plan was to drive to Chicago with Jessie and visit Bobbi before heading to the East Coast. We had kept in touch continually that year. I planned on staying with her at her parents' house during my visit. She had gotten a white dog in Arizona as well, and we were always hanging out together. We all were really looking forward to this planned visit that was going to be the epitome of youthful exuberance and disco flash that was the mid-1970's. Jessie and I showed up all dirty and funky from our drive to appear at the palatial home of Bobbi's parents in the affluent north suburb of Chicago: Wilmette, IL. I think just having my beat-up van parked at their house must have embarrassed them with the neighbors, not to mention the oil leaking from it onto their driveway. Bobbi and I were so glad to see each other, and I got along great with her folks. I can still feel those big soft bath towels hanging by the bathtub and see their housekeeper taking care of things. It was an experience that was completely foreign to me.

We got high and played in her pool all day, then got together with her friends in the evening. I stayed a couple of weeks, and it was like a high-end vacation like I had never experienced. I was on yet another new independent adventure, but I was also having strong feelings for Bobbi. I knew I was leaving soon and starting a new life, but I couldn't help but acknowledge the emotions that were definitely affecting me. I realized I had a real romantic attraction to Bobbi. I had sexual experiences in high school, but it wasn't mature in any way. This, though, felt mature. It was the first time that I saw that we could really be both friends and lovers. In her, I found somebody where I could be comfortable. I could be myself.

Bobbi's childhood boyfriend, now a close friend of mine, who she planned on marrying, lived with his parents just a few blocks away. We had all been going out together that first week and reliving our Tucson party life. One evening I got a call from him asking if I would want to go for a ride with him and smoke a joint. Not knowing what Bobbi had planned, and it being the early evening, I said sure and went out to meet him at the curb in front of Bobbi's house. I jumped in his car, and we took a spin around the neighborhood getting high. When we pulled back up in front of Bobbi's house, he asked me to stay in the car as he had something that he wanted to talk to me about. Being stoned, I don't remember the exact words or how it started, but despite my affected brain I do remember what was said. He proceeded to tell me that he was in love with me. He had feelings for me that had been holed up inside of him since we first met. Now, I am an open person, and I have no issues with anyone's sexuality. But this threw me so off guard that I wasn't sure what to do. I think I must have given him some definitive non-encouragement but also let him know that it was all cool. After going back into Bobbi's house, I was confused as to how to handle my own feelings for Bobbi, her belief and feelings for him, and now his feelings and coming out to me. I knew for sure though that it was time to leave Chicago and be on my way.

Bobbi eventually broke up with her boyfriend, who on my road trip stopover I'm pretty sure had confided that he was actually in love with me, despite his marriage plans with Bobbi. I never spoke about it with her, and to this day I'm not entirely sure why they broke up. But after starting my new life in Rhode Island, I knew from our conversations that Bobbi and I were destined to be together. And I was happy about it. Apparently, all our lives were in transition, and I was now living an artist's life far from the life of luxury that I had experienced in the suburbs of Chicago.

I began my semester at RISD and started seeing another girl. But my relationship with Bobbi continued on the phone. After a lot of back-and-forth conversation and Bobbi deciding to transfer school to Boston, we connected in Providence. Upon Bobbi's arrival, we gave into our feelings for each other, but unfortunately my girlfriend came home and caught us. She walked right in on us in bed. That was clearly a not so nice end to my romantic relationship with my girlfriend. I wasn't proud of how things ended between us, and it gave me a lot of guilt. It was wrong, but I was in love with Bobbi and quickly moved on. Months later my now ex-girlfriend was making out with a new boyfriend in a running parked car after a winter night's date and they both died of asphyxiation, which became front-page news in the small town of Providence. My guilt in how I had treated her became a depressing awareness of a potential character flaw that bothered me incessantly. This lurid story haunted me through my time at school.

Bobbi had moved to Boston to attend Emerson College, a 45-minute drive from Providence. Bobbi and I instantly became a couple, and after transferring to Emerson College, we both commuted back and forth seeing each other constantly. At Emerson, she began to curate her own makeup program that leaped over the theatrical makeup curriculum and into the fashion and beauty industry. *To this day, she's still credited with being the founder of this makeup program at Emerson.* Little did I know that Bobbi and I would get even closer soon enough, and we would both find ourselves on upward career trajectories.

Chapter 4
Model Photographer

Although still in school, it seemed a new career was on the horizon for me. Bobbi's stepdad coincidentally had a photography business with photographers around the country shooting portfolios for young women in various modeling schools. They would travel to photograph hundreds of would-be models and then sell the pictures to their parents. It was quantity over quality, so different from what I was learning at art school, but I was up for the job when he offered it to me. He introduced me to one of the photographers to apprentice with, a fun, always tanned guy who wore turquoise jewelry and cowboy boots and had a girlfriend in every city and always had a ton of weed. *This was the life for me*, I thought.

At 20 years old, I began working part-time and picked up a few of his local accounts. This weird niche industry started to interest me, and although I was in school full time, I managed this double life of traveling, partying, constantly meeting new people, and learning how to shoot pictures in a fast-paced commercial setting. My art school wasn't teaching students how to actually make a living in photography, so this became an odd balance.

Bobbi's dad showed me how to make money while learning how to make art. All of a sudden, I had a business, cameras, and equipment supplied by Bobbi's stepdad as well as unlimited access to film and strobe lights. I drove Bobbi's brand-new Thunderbird up and down the East Coast, traveling to each modeling school. I picked up a ton of accounts. I was taking photos of girls ages 11 through 25, photographing 50 to 75 girls per day, 150 sessions per month. I was learning ten times more than in my college classes and earning a ton of money.

During these sessions, I not only became the star in the room, but hyper-mindful of my clientele: Young girls who were looking to find their inner confidence and have it projected onto my lens. They worshipped photos of supermodels who were much older than them in their favorite magazines, yet still wanted to emulate them to a T. Yet adolescence wasn't always the kindest to this age group: Acne, braces, awkwardness in their own, growing skin. The control I needed to have in the room, at that time, was one of making them feel comfortable, to be an understanding ear that this wasn't easy for them. I used my charm and came up with some witty banter to make them feel at ease. I considered what they would want to talk about or think about during the shoot.

The truth was, I was just as awkward as they were; I was just better at pretending that I had full control of the room. I set up my seamless paper and put up the strobe lights. I directed each aspiring model, telling them how to move and relate to the camera, all the while keeping the flow of talking and having fun in the mix. Whatever language it took to keep them engaged.

"Oh my God, this looks amazing!" I would say, and I meant it, but I probably put on a little more ebullient charm that a tween girl may have recognized more than an adult.

Another one: "Oh, I love those shoes!"

Then I'd let them feel as though they were having the full supermodel experience: "Let me give you more of a jawline!"

In the end, I treated these 13-year-olds with acne and growing pains like they were any other supermodel on the runway. I wanted them to feel good about themselves. My job was to help them mature; what I thought at the time was that I could make you feel confident in yourself. It was the beginning of what I would come to do with celebrities: Making them feel more like themselves in front of the camera. It was an *empowering* rather than a *powering* move, making them feel like they were acting out the vision they had of themselves in their head. I would also pose and show them how to give supermodel angles. I just kept going and talking and distracted them from their own nerves. This banter distracted my subjects so I could find something in them that would make them look and feel good about themselves and the photoshoot overall.

I had to make them comfortable to get the best pictures. It built up my natural confidence in already knowing how to talk to people and allowed me to get them to respond and trust me. At the same time, I was learning at such a fast pace. This time of my life was incredibly important in the development of who I was and who I would become later on as a celebrity photographer.

As my career would skyrocket in later years, I would use these same techniques when I photographed the Hollywood elite and political dignitaries that would become the definition of my career. In Bobbi's stepdad's business, I learned my game by shooting these aspiring models. The pace and breadth of jobs was unbelievable, and I reveled in the experience.

In my senior year of college, my thesis project culminated in an exhibition. No class was necessary, and I just had to meet with my professors once a week. Given this additional freedom, I rented a duplex brownstone apartment with a rooftop in Boston so I could spend more time with Bobbi. I was only 22 years old and already living this rich life. I started traveling regularly, either on the road shooting models or down to school in Providence. My dog Jessie had seven puppies at this time, and I'd put them all in a brown box in the Thunderbird and commuted to Providence once a week for my school meetings. In between, I worked on shooting pictures and spending time in the darkroom making prints for my thesis project.

My exhibition went beautifully, and Bobbi and I both graduated. We stayed in Boston for the summer, deciding our next move. I was still working the modeling school's connections, and I got a taste for making money in photography. I liked having an elevated, "go-go-go" accelerated approach to everything I did and had, including a nice apartment and car, and a healthy expense account. At this point, Bobbi and I were trying to figure out our lives together. She had done so well in college, but she had her own interests beyond that theatrical style of makeup and didn't want to do prosthetic noses and wigs for the theater for the rest of her career. She wanted to do makeup for the models and stars shown in *Vogue* and the upper level of fashion and celebrity. The time was right for both of us to move to NYC.

Chapter 5
Positively 4th St

When we made the big move to New York City, Bobbi and I found ourselves growing professionally in our own ways. It was during the '80s, and the fashion, music and movie scenes were all colliding, especially when it came to photography. We rented an apartment across from the iconic Fedora restaurant on W. 4th St. in the West Village. In 1980, I collaborated with my best friend from high school and roommate from college, *also photographers*, to rent a loft that needed a lot of work in midtown, just above Chelsea on 29th St. between 6th and 7th Avenues. It was once a building of sweatshops, which we gutted and turned into a photo studio. We didn't have any real money to now live in NYC and with a photo studio as well. My sole income was still coming from my modeling school gigs. I brought my one friend along to the modeling sessions so we could double our accounts and workload, and eventually I could hand off my camera to him so I could pursue more work in the city. I remember riding my bicycle down Fashion (7th) Avenue, a portfolio cradled under my arm as I pedaled like a maniac to get around the city, dropping off my work and looking for jobs that would take me to the next level of my career.

As Bobbi started working her way through the fashion industry in New York City, she introduced me to a very creative commercial photographer friend named Chris Callis, who after hanging out and getting to know each other, asked me to be his photography assistant on the album cover and fashion industry shoots he did on location and in his studio. This was a major connection for me and was my entrée into bigger and better photography opportunities. I started to learn even more at a much higher level of photography and found myself capable of seeing my future career at another level. We worked on many fashion shoots, celebrity portraits, and album covers. I actually shot an early Bon Jovi album cover with Chris that would precede my long, successful relationship with the band.

Chris opened up a world to me, and I started working with him full time. I ended up spending zero time at the loft I had renovated with my friends. I was crossing over into

Bobbi's world of fashion, advertising, and magazine work. I was fast forwarding from model school photographer to the top of New York City commercial and art photography world. I began shooting for music magazines and small portrait shoots for *Vogue*, *Harper's Bazaar*, and other high-end magazines. My portfolio grew and had the right combination of cool, funky, creative, and commercial. This was the melding of art and commerce, which perfectly reflected what I learned in art school and on the job.

Besides the obvious career boost for Bobbi and me, living in the West Village was also a personal adventure unto itself. At the time, this famed neighborhood was quirky and filled with unique characters milling around our small apartment on West Fourth Street between 10th and Charles. We were very social people and had a lot of great friends and relationships and often had people over to our house, which was small and roach infested, but our first New York City apartment together out of college. One evening I heard a commotion out in the hallway. Our apartment was on the first floor all the way down the end, straight ahead from the front door. If you looked out the peep hole, you could see who was in the lobby. I heard a commotion, opened up our front door to find two young men beating on an old man who was on the floor in our lobby just behind the glass door that separated the lobby from our hallway.

I immediately became incensed and yelled, "Hey, stop that! Get off that guy!" They ignored me and so I ran out my door and down the hallway toward the lobby. As I quickly ran toward them, they saw me and ran out of the building. I threw open the heavy glass door and put my hand on the old man's back who was on his knees and said, "Are you okay?"

And he mumbled something, but I just took off instinctively. As I ran after these two men, I jumped down the stairs and turned the corner onto West Fourth Street as I saw them turn right onto West 10th.

It was November and chilly and I only had a t-shirt on, but I was fully engaged in chasing these two individuals. I always had a very soft spot in my heart for old people and was very close with my grandmother before her death, so the fact that they had hurt this old man made me so angry that I blindly continued the chase. As I ran at full speed down West 10th Street, I was starting to catch up with them. I was a daily runner, and being someone who is in good shape and a runner of races, my pace was in full stride. As I started to catch up, I noticed there was a row of garbage cans all along the sidewalk on West 10th Street, and I quickly grabbed a garbage can cover for protection against the fact that I might catch up with these two guys and that they may have a weapon or in some way turn on me.

It didn't deter me though, and I kept on after grabbing the cover and as I came up on Bleeker Street, I was sure they would split up and go in different directions. That would have been the smart thing to do, but instead they foolishly stayed together and took a left on Bleecker heading into Seventh Avenue and Christopher Street, toward Sheridan Square. I turned the corner, still running at full speed after them holding this garbage can cover with no jacket on. Sheridan Square was full of people, and I must have looked like a lunatic, and in fact, I probably looked like the criminal instead of the two people I was chasing.

As we got to Seventh Avenue, they quickly jumped into an available cab and took off. I ran across Seventh Avenue to a police car that was parked with two policemen sitting in the front seat, drinking coffee and minding their post. They must have been astonished and probably had a hand on their guns as I quickly approached their car with the garbage can cover in full stride. I must have looked like an insane gladiator, but typical of NYC cops, they casually rolled down the window to hear what I was about, and I breathlessly said, "Those two guys, they just robbed a man, and they jumped into that cab!"

They said, "Get in!" I jumped in the back of their car and with the siren blasting we chased the taxi down Seventh Avenue.

We managed to pull it over and the cops with guns drawn, dragged the two perpetrators out of the backseat and threw them against the car based on my insistence of witnessing their criminal behavior. They put them in cuffs, and we all got into the police car and drove to the West Village Police Station. On arrival at the station, we walked in to find that the old man had already been escorted to the police station by someone. I'm not sure if that was a neighbor or maybe he was there by himself, but he was bruised and shaken with a dried trickle of blood coming down his mouth where the men had apparently beaten him. When we got into the station, the police were agitated and as disturbed as I was that these two young men had attacked such a seemingly feeble old man. To move the story further along, the guys were both arrested and the old man was taken care of and sent on his way.

The next day I got a phone call from a police detective with the Career Criminal Unit with the New York City Police Department. He asked if he could take me to lunch and have a conversation with me. I agreed. Over the course of the lunch, he told me that these two were career criminals and that his job was to put them away. They definitely attacked this old man and I was the witness. He asked if I would testify before a grand jury, and if so, it would guarantee these young men would pay for their crime.

I said yes, and over the course of the next two weeks before the grand jury hearing date was scheduled, he continued to keep in touch with me, meet me, and generally make sure that I was willing to complete what I had agreed to do and to befriend me in a way that made me feel like I was doing the right thing. This went on until the grand jury hearing, where I showed up and gave my testimony. Apparently these two men were convicted of their crime and went to prison, but *The Daily News* had heard about the arrest and my chasing these bandits through the street. They interviewed me and did a story in the magazine with a photo of me and a headline on the article that said, "Two Suspects Get Trashed."

The recognition was funny and I was very shy about it, but on the other hand it was kind of great and something I was proud of. I talked in the article about how important my grandmother was to me and that I was really offended by the fact that these two young men bullied and beat on an old man. Surprisingly, *The Daily News* ran a follow up piece, and I was on a list for a program that the news outlet called, "Hero of the Week," where they honored a New Yorker who did something heroic and gave out a thousand dollars award.

Well, I won the award and was made Hero of the Week. It all felt so weird to me having recognition for something that I just instinctively did. They had a ceremony where I was then given the award at a police station in midtown Manhattan and President Reagan came to give me the award. My father came into the city and watched proudly as I was given this honor by the president of the United States. The funny thing is, I was just this young hippie guy with long hair and was probably smoking a joint and stoned in my apartment when I heard the noise in the lobby, but I did what I thought was right and stuck to my guns. I'll not only never forget the incident, but the recognition and the feeling that I knew what was right. Despite my irreverent and alternative approach to life, I was a righteous guy who had the integrity that my father had taught me. I had not only accomplished a good Samaritan task, and then accepted an award and recognition for it, but I had the opportunity to share that moment with my dad.

By the mid-1980s, both Bobbi and I had major careers. I started working on more and more music and celebrity shoots. I started to get small magazine assignments shooting new bands and young Hollywood celebs such as Elvis Costello, Duran Duran, and a young Johnny Depp. I then started flying back and forth to LA on cheap $100 flights and knocked on the doors of Hollywood record companies and movie studios, getting appointments with art and marketing directors and asking for work. Things started moving quickly and I was soon getting a lot of work and developing a name on the West Coast. I'm not sure why, but it just clicked. I guess I had a cute confidence and charisma that got me in the door where I let them know that I knew what I wanted. Then my first real personal celebrity connection came with a photoshoot with Julian Lennon, John Lennon's oldest son. I was hired by his record company to do publicity shots for a music video he was filming. We were both young and at similar places in our careers, and we just hit it off. I eventually shot two of his albums and we became friends. We were comfortable around each other, and we both seemed to want to share in each other's creative opportunities. My hustle earned me an LA agent who started working hard on my behalf. He got me into the lucrative movie poster business. I soon became the go-to person for doing these Hollywood advertising campaigns and movie posters – such as *Home Alone*, *Groundhog Day*, *Sleepless in Seattle*, *Bad Santa*, and *Tommy Boy*, to name a few. It was challenging work that was lucrative beyond what I thought possible at the time. I loved that I had entered this world of Hollywood where I could be a part of and contribute to the film business. I had self-assuredness that made my subject and my client feel good, and I could come through with the pictures and make everyone happy.

But inside, I didn't necessarily have the same level of confidence.

My ego and work ethic carried through each shoot, but there was a sense that I was pulling something over on everyone. Was it imposter syndrome?

As my career started to take off, Bobbi and I decided to leave our small apartment in the village and rent a loft in Hell's Kitchen, back before gentrification changed the whole neighborhood. We found ourselves in this isolated old factory building on 10th Ave and 37th Street overlooking the Lincoln Tunnel. The neighborhood hadn't turned yet; it was the Wild West. We lived in the space, I used it as my studio, and Bobbi did her photoshoots with other photographers during the day around the city. We were starting to build a life where we were publicly recognized as an up-and-coming power couple in the business. *Glamour* magazine profiled us, which probably came from Bobbi's growing success in the business and the fact that we were both becoming visible. Legendary photographer Patrick Demarchelier photographed us. This was a big moment, and we were just kids.

By 1984, Bobbi and I were becoming masters of our domain, but we were personally going in different directions. She wanted to get married and have children. As great as our relationship was, from friendship to love to partnership, I needed to live a life that felt free to go where my career would take me. I was 28 years old, needed to keep the doors open, and felt that a marriage and family at that time would root me to a place. I didn't want to freeze any part of my life and potential opportunities. We had known each other for 10 years at this point, and while it was painful to split from Bobbi, we broke up for the best. She ended up getting married and having children with someone else, and that was OK. I was on my own and had everything I needed. Besides, my career was about to take on new heights.

Chapter 6
Working with Whoopi

In 1984, I was deep in the social scene of New York City. Any night of the week, you could find me at openings, parties and gatherings. I met tons of people, often dancing into the wee morning hours at the height of the city's disco scene. I was climbing up the ladder of my career, getting invited to events and meeting the right people while passing spoons under our noses to do a bump or two of cocaine on the dance floor. One of those heady nights, I was invited to see Whoopi Goldberg in her groundbreaking one-woman show. The future EGOT-winner's incredible performance in *Direct from Broadway* changed my life. Little did I know that we'd eventually share a friendship that has spanned over thirty years.

Sitting in the audience that night, I was blown away. She was so brilliant and hip. I'll never forget it. My seats were good and I had a perfect view. I remember the power I felt in this woman pacing alone on this big stage and in total control. She played multiple characters, all with different personalities: A junkie, a Valley Girl, a Jamaican woman, a young disabled person and even her young daughter, donning a long-sleeved cream-hued shirt with the arms dangling around her face as if it was "long luxurious blonde hair." Her irreverent performance as a soon-to-be seven-year-old girl made the audience roar with laughter and, in her deftly quiet moments, consider how society prioritizes whiteness over the Black experience.

Whoopi's personal, unique comedic voice was unlike anything I had ever seen before or since. Her performance left such an impression on me, and I was immediately stricken with a feeling of seeing an open and honest creative, bursting forward with something new and different. She wasn't afraid to "go there." As someone who was working his way up the career ladder, I was awed and inspired to hold the attention of a room like Whoopi. While stepping out of the theater amongst the sold-out crowd, I wondered what it'd be like to exude her brand of confidence in my own photoshoots, which I felt like I did, yet I often wondered if my outside matched my insides.

Coincidentally or not, a few years later, I was hired to shoot Whoopi for a magazine layout. Not only was I able to meet and collaborate with someone who was on top of her game, but we hit it off immediately. I guess we both were at a unique place, and it just clicked. Whoopi came to the set looking great in jeans and a black top. We had a few outfits for her that the stylist brought, and I remember one billowy black caftan that had this amazing fluid shape when she moved. I started shooting one photo after another, having my assistants swap out cameras and different film, depending on the look I was going for. To her credit, Whoopi was up for anything. At one point, she stood in the frame of a closed-up window in the studio. "Get up there," I said, and she balanced herself on this small ledge wearing this long black dress. As she moved her body, with her head down and her dreads flowing, the dress took on such a beautiful shape within the white window frame as I saw the shot come together.

Then we headed to the rooftop for another look, this time against the Manhattan skyline. There was a dark patinaed corrugated metal wall that I asked her to stand in front of. And then Whoopi surprised me. She asked me to take a photo of her from behind. That is certainly not something an actor would usually request. I obliged and took the picture and immediately realized what a great portrait it was. The photo was definitely, definitively Whoopi, and anyone looking at the photo would instantly know who it was. She taught me something that day about creativity, and she's been teaching me ever since.

At the end of the shoot and at my usual pace, I followed Whoopi out to the street as she was about to drive away. I quickly hailed a cab and asked the driver to just keep his cab in the middle of the street and allow me to use the car as a hired prop. The final photo of this shoot was Whoopi perched on the hood of the cab, the perfect combination of her upfront New York personality and the creative use of the landscape and a quick moment in time. Once we wrapped, she stepped off the taxi, said goodbye and got into her waiting limo. I took photos of my subject right up until the moment she had to leave. My economy of time with each subject, particularly Whoopi in this moment, built our friendship.

What does it take to get the shot? Not much with an incredible subject like Whoopi and New York City as the backdrop. Even when it is a photo of Whoopi from behind, with only the back of her shirt and her dreads, it can become iconic. We'd go onto many other shoots together, whether publicity for the Oscars, a movie poster, or some advertising campaign.

Throughout the years, as we were growing together in our respective careers, we became closer as friends.

Whoopi and I together always felt right. The electricity that bonded us as creative collaborators and then close friends became something more over the years. By 1988, Bobbi and I had long gone our separate ways, and I had eloped with a beautiful ballerina named Elicia. *More on how Elicia and I met in the next chapter*. She was 12 years younger than me and existed in a different world entirely. While I built up our relationship to be a storybook romance, I knew in my heart that it wasn't. Yes, I loved Elicia, and yet I preferred Whoopi's company most of the time. Whoopi and I were born in the same year, were both smart and snappy and shared this incredible connection that often didn't have a title. It was just warm, exciting and fulfilling.

Without fully realizing it, my burgeoning feelings were the foreshadowing of a crush. We were already into each other's lives, and I became a staple at her family events: July 4th, Christmas, you name it. My portraits of her dotted the house. Although I never publicly named it before now, I found myself deep down the well, thinking over and over again, "Could this be a real feeling, and if so, what's it based on?" While I was always faithful in my marriage, my feelings about Whoopi at this time were often in my thoughts.

At one of our shoots, her longtime producer said, "She adores you." He'd said this many times but probably not in the context of what I was feeling. I was curious...did Whoopi and I feel the same way? Perhaps she was asking herself the same questions I was? My crush on a dear friend seemed mutual. We never talked about it, though, and no other action was taken. I was loyal to my wife, but if Whoopi and I hadn't been married to different people at the time, I would have asked her out.

This spark eventually receded with time and inaction. Yet the blueprint of a platonically romantic friendship lingers. I always greet her with a kiss on the back of her head, nuzzling her hair and hugging her from behind. We talk almost every other week about the most important and trivial things going on in our lives. We've even jokingly agreed we would retire to a little island in the Mediterranean together when we're old and to watch the ocean ebb and flow from our dueling lounge chairs.

After this moment, we continued working together on photoshoots and creative projects. One of these memorable shots came from a real-life experience where Whoopi was sitting in a women's restroom stall in Las Vegas when a fan in the next stall passed her a piece of toilet tissue and asked for her autograph. Amazingly, she signed it and handed it back. The moment became the perfect idea for a shot and one that fit both our comedic sensibilities.

We recreated the photo in the restroom of a theater where we were shooting at, and the person playing the autograph-seeker was ironically my wife at the time, or at least her sandal and hand holding the pen and "paper". Whoopi's expression in the black-and-white photo showed the perfect range of emotions: Incredulousness, surprise, wondering, "Can you believe this chick?" all in one expression like only Whoopi can.

One day Whoopi called me and said she needed us to collaborate on an advertising campaign because she felt the client didn't have a clue on how to make it great and that the two of us needed to take charge. She said that it was for a feminine product, a napkin for something they called "light bladder leakage."

This was a subject I had no personal experience with. Apparently, one in three women experienced "a little sprinkle" when they laughed, were tickled, or startled. We talked at length on the phone about how, if one in three women have this issue, then that could be anyone, and perhaps it was something that has always happened to women, including women throughout history. What better person to promote this product than someone who could make you pee in your pants anyway?

The producers on the commercial wanted to use a plain green screen backdrop and direct her, which would mean a full script. This wasn't her style, which I knew the moment she laid out their plan. Always ready to jump into Whoopi's world, we started brainstorming about how we could make this ad great. I needed to not only promote a product, but to give free rein for her incredible mind to improvise. As she and I came up with ideas that would make this campaign a series of characters, I realized that what we envisioned could be an expensive shoot that this client did not have the budget for. I needed to do both a print campaign as well as direct a commercial, and I had to make it all work. I took my years of experience in still photography and my ability to create an illusion out of basically nothing and applied it to this production. I used simple painted backdrops, and a collection of rented props and costumes to create a scene for Whoopi and her characters to inhabit.

"How about the Mona Lisa?" said Whoopi.

"Well, the Mona Lisa isn't a real person," I said, "but there was a model who posed for the Mona Lisa!"

We came up with a list of names. I went back to the advertising people and showed them our ideas for the model who posed for the sculpture of the Statue of Liberty, the Princess and the Pea, Cleopatra...funny characters and things that she could just riff off of. I quickly gathered a team of costume designers, set designers and assistants, and we booked a studio and put together a full-on video commercial crew. Then we got to work building the sets that applied to each of the characters, no green screens allowed. I had such little money for the ad, but I was determined.

The shoot was scheduled to take two days, and after her morning taping of *The View*, Whoopi would spend two hours each day filming the commercial and taking the photos with me. On my shoestring budget, I created an illusion with lighting and props that had a sense of reality but veered into fantasy. In this sense, we knew it was fake, which made it so funny. In one, we featured Whoopi as Eve from Adam and Eve in the Garden of Eden standing in a lush forest backdrop. We put fake plants all around her, and she appeared as though she was naked and wearing a long blonde wig—a hilarious callback to "this is my long, luxurious blonde hair." With the right lighting and lens, she popped out of the greenery. There was no copy, no direction, and we planned to let her ad-lib just using the environment. Whoopi would do the rest. When she was dressed as the Mona Lisa, she said in a hysterically funny Italian accent, "I don't want to be painted, I want to be dry!" We all needed a Poise pad on the set after she started cracking us up, but we had to keep it together because we knew Whoopi's spontaneity and timing only allowed for a few takes.

One character she played was Joan of Arc. For this set, I built a rustic platform and tree trunk coming out of it with an over-the-top thick rope.

We tied her to the fake stake and had a short wig and Joan of Arc-like clothing. A special effects guy had the smallest smoke machine that wafted up and around her legs. It was all so funny as these little bursts of smoke appeared beneath her and with every take the viewer got the joke that her leaking kept the stake from burning. She just giggled on set as I directed her video and concurrently then did stills. Then, for the Princess and the Pea character, we placed 15 mattresses on top of each other, and to make them stack safely we had this steel armature placed through the pile for stability so she could just climb up on top of them and be secure. It was a simple set, placed in the corner of a room we built that looked like castle walls. Fake but effective. She was in her damsel costume that personified the Princess and the Pea to a "T." I developed this fast pace and kept the energy high on set as she walked up the ladder to sit on top of these mattresses. She startled us all on the first take as she began speaking in a deep-voiced Brooklyn accent, craggy like a chain smoker. We were all trying to keep from laughing and not blow the take, since she was sitting precariously up in the air ad-libbing and clearly on a roll. I gave her the context, and she gave us back a fully-fledged, funny character. There was also a Cleopatra character sitting at the end of a long Egyptian-like table talking about Poise, a model posing in an art studio as the Statue of Liberty speaking in a French accent, and Lady Godiva with a wig that hit the floor as she sat on a fake, life-size horse. We weren't prepared for anything she said, and that was the most fun part of it. It created such a dynamic campaign for the company that they ended up buying commercial time during the Oscars broadcast, which is such a high dollar commercial spot like the Super Bowl that they felt warranted the expense. It was a surprisingly big shoot, and Whoopi was happy.

Whoopi gave me such freedom through our collaborations on shoots, and that allowed me to expand my own creativity and to do it with someone I love and revere so much. Whenever she has some kind of charity event, I am always there to help her and vice versa. She can call me for anything she needs and I am there. We've worked together for over 30 years, and I was, and still am, proud of our collaborations and our ability to create incredible images that have had an indelible impact on pop culture.

Whoopi has never been afraid to reveal herself in front of the camera, and yet, has always done it on her own terms. In one shoot, she showed off her shoulder tattoo, which she had never before revealed. Always authentic, and being herself, once for a Weight Watchers campaign she stood again with her back to the camera, and an oversized bra slung over her shoulder indicating how much weight she had lost on the diet program. This "shot from behind thing" we do which features only her back and her dreads, has become something we do on every shoot.

Our friendship has always been one of mutual support. In May 2021, I was sitting in my home office, vacillating between booking another flight to see my elderly mother in New Jersey, *who I'd already just seen the week before*, or staying home another week before making a second trip. She had been suffering from dementia and now had a scary infection that did not make me feel right. She had recently been in and out of the hospital. I called Whoopi and told her my feelings. After a long silence, which was very unlike our usual banter, she spoke firmly and lovingly to my heart.

"You know what to do," she said, and hung up the phone.

I booked a flight and ran to the airport within the hour for a flight from California to New Jersey. As I'll talk about more a little later, I got to hold my mom's hand and say goodbye to her. Without Whoopi's thoughtful tough love on the phone that afternoon, I wouldn't have experienced the peace that I would feel if I hadn't rushed to my mom's bedside that night as she passed away not long after I arrived. Afterward, I stayed at Whoopi's home as I planned my mother's memorial service, and all of the things that come with saying goodbye to a loved one.

For me, our relationship can be summarized best when I was inducted into the New Jersey Hall of Fame. Whoopi, a fellow New Jersey resident, gave a speech on my behalf. She stood at the podium and said, "This is an extraordinary man who I adore and have adored for thirty-some-odd years. He's incredibly talented and one of the great 'eyes' on the planet." After a video montage of my work played, I walked up the stairs and embraced her. I shared with the audience how important our relationship is and that "I've shared more fun, more laughter, great work and a lot of love from this very special human being." Mic drop.

Chapter 7

A South America Trip

When I first arrived in New York City, I befriended a brilliant Venezuelan artist named Rafael Bogarin, an abstract painter who gave me a new perspective on my photography. His wife was a friend of my sister, and we immediately hit it off. We started hanging out late into the night, talking about art and experimental styles of photography.

Rafael was doing a big art project in Venezuela and invited me to join. The government was paying for his project, which was to gather twenty-five artists from different countries around the world to paint murals along a deserted stretch of highway. The idea was to bring art to people who normally wouldn't be exposed to the fine art world. He called it *Arte' Vial*...or highway art. This would be my first international trip in my life, and I was game. I traveled to Venezuela for the first time with Rafael, and it was a transformative experience.

When I returned to New York City, I connected with another artist from that project, a well-known Colombian painter named Omar Rayo, who was also friends with Rafael. Omar, a successful artist, had his own museum in Roldanillo, Colombia, the small town where he grew up. At that time, in 1981, the town was an old, rough village surrounded by farms that grew corn and cotton. The streets were barely paved. The stucco buildings were weathered and worn, something out of an old Clint Eastwood western shot in Mexico. Right in the middle of this scene sat this white, modern, beautiful museum dedicated to their most famous resident.

Omar and I connected on the Venezuelan shoot, as I did with some of the other artists. Somehow I was offered the chance to come down to Colombia and work on a similar project he was developing. At that time, Venezuela and Colombia, although neighboring countries, were still politically opposed, or at least not as friendly as they could be. Omar and Rafael came up with an idea to do another highway museum. They would invite artists from their respective countries and create it on the border between Venezuela and Colombia. The project was meant to represent a larger collaboration and friendship between the two countries.

The outdoor museum was to be built near a bridge crossing a large river that served as the border. The artwork would be split on either side of the bridge, half in Colombia and half in Venezuela. It was a striking metaphor: A bridge between countries, done as a peaceful, uniting gesture. I was finishing one project in Venezuela and stepping into another, very similar one, now under Omar's direction. At the end of the project, I had the opportunity to meet both the presidents of Venezuela and Colombia. Here I was, this kid from New Jersey who was a long way from home, standing in the middle of a bridge between two foreign countries and shaking hands with both presidents.

I couldn't help but reflect on suddenly becoming an international traveler. Clearly, I was a long way from Jersey and New York City: Here I was, this kid just out of college, working on not one, but two incredible projects in South America. I had befriended all of these people who treated me with reverence and respect, as if I were a real artist and journalist. At 22 years old, I was connecting with unique, older, and more successful artists from a completely different part of the world. I had barely done any traveling, never mind being out of the country or in such an exotic place. But there I was, traveling to South America with this feeling of excitement and anticipation for everything in front of me.

While I was there doing these art-related projects, I was also shooting everything for myself. I was building a library of images as part of my stock portfolio: cars, cactuses, animals, street scenes, cultural festivities. Parties, people dancing, bars, restaurants. Wherever I was, I was shooting everything and organizing it into categories.

Another Colombian artist I met on the first project in Venezuela, who was also part of the joint country project, was named Edgar Correal. Edgar invited me to come back and visit him in Bogotá. He was young and slight, very sweet, and he invited me to stay with him. His paintings reflected his personality; soft colors and beautiful, natural forms, and animal elements like birds.

At that point, I had gotten an assignment to photograph Colombian artists. I was using these new relationships, and my growing comfort traveling in South America, to push my career in New York. I was positioning myself as someone who could work on another continent. As I started going back and forth more often, I was doing anything I could to move my career forward. I saw how people responded to my "exotic" travel, so I chased assignments, made good money as a photographer, and kept shooting constantly.

On each trip, I'd go around to all kinds of magazines in New York: A family magazine, a sports magazine, an auto publication, anything. I would convince them that on my next trip to South America and say I could shoot something for them. I could give them worldly, expensive-looking production value just by creating an assignment myself. Most of the time, the magazines loved it and were more than willing to agree to the assignment. I was such a hustler. I was getting all these magazines and people to trust me, while I was just going down to another continent with that kind of naïveté and somehow pulling it off.

In particular, I remember convincing the editor of *Parents* magazine, who did children's fashion layouts, to give me a suitcase filled with kids' clothes and take them to South America. Once there, I created a fashion story. The parents of children in a small town in the Andes Mountains agreed to the shoot with their kids – especially when I said they could keep the clothes (which was great since I then didn't have to bring the clothes back in my suitcase).

Then I photographed these kids dressed in these clothes, amongst beautiful, dynamic landscapes. I staged these incredible scenes: Kids walking down a path with a donkey on a leash, in the mountains, wearing raincoats and boots or whatever the magazine had sent.

On this particular trip, a magazine asked me to do a story on a group of artists who lived in Bogotá. So I made arrangements to go there. I contacted Edgar and asked if I could stay with him. He barely spoke English, in fact very little, and I spoke very little Spanish. But I stayed at his house, and somehow we communicated. We had a really unique time. I'll never forget the experience.

Edgar was a trippy, quiet, gentle little man, and he lived his life in a simple, bohemian way. Staying with him was something completely new for me. I was young and alone, yet I felt so confident and open to everything that was happening. And again, I photographed everything. I always had my cameras. I always had hundreds of rolls of slide film with me.

After doing these pictures, Edgar wanted to take me on an excursion that would eventually bring us to Omar's town of Roldanillo. We traveled from Bogotá over the Andes toward a town called Manizales, about halfway through the trip, where we would spend the night. To get there, it was about a 24-hour drive. It was a serious trek.

We drove in his little Jeep over the mountains, and at some point we pulled into a small village. We stopped, and these little kids came over to the Jeep. Edgar said something to them in Spanish, and they came back with these large, fresh mushroom caps, which Edgar and I proceeded to eat.

Edgar and I had smoked weed together before, so I knew the mushrooms were psilocybin. We proceeded to get very, very high. There I was with this skinny, bald, dark-skinned man, physically similar to Gandhi, except with a scruffy beard.

We drove a short distance out of town, somewhere Edgar clearly knew, down some dirt paths that led us to a slow-moving river. The landscape was desolate and beautiful. We pulled up, got out, and went for a swim. The midday sun was strong and hot, and we were starting to feel the effects. By the time we got to the river, we jumped in. We felt like we were flying. I had done hallucinogens before, a lot of experimenting in high school, LSD, mescaline, all of it. But this was different. It was more intense. Maybe it was the setting. Maybe it was the moment. I don't even remember if I had done psilocybin like this before.

While we were in the river, these kids were playing on a rope hanging from a tree. They were swinging out and splashing down into the water. We joined them, sharing in their joy as we kept buzzing. I barely spoke Spanish. I understood even less, especially being that high. But it didn't matter. We laughed. We communicated in some other way. We had our own language. I'll never forget how the light reflected off the water, refracting, glittering in my eyes as I photographed Edgar and the kids. I photographed him and the children jumping, laughing, splashing into the river, completely alive in that moment. Everything felt beautiful.

Of course, it was exaggerated by the psilocybin.

I didn't know that at the time.

After a couple of hours, we walked back to the Jeep. Then, all of a sudden, I saw it. A double rainbow stretching across the sky. I was completely immersed in it. Fumbling with my cameras, shooting like crazy. Kodachrome loaded. I was losing my mind at the beauty of what I was seeing, what I felt like I was living.

I'll never forget getting back to New York, so excited to see the film. Only to find the images were...just kind of banal. The drug played a trick on me. It was just a standard picture of a rainbow. Beautiful, sure, especially in that setting, but nowhere near what my tripped-out brain had experienced.

After this illusory stopover in the mountains, we arrived in Roldanillo, in the Cauca Valley. Edgar and I went to meet Omar and see his museum. It was a beautiful little town, and I photographed everything and everyone I met. I remember sitting in cafes and walking down the streets, passing broken-down adobe houses and kids playing in the alleys. Donkeys and horses were everywhere. Stray dogs filled the streets. It felt like something out of a dream. Very little was modern. Even the cars were old. It reminded me of what we now think of as Cuba, frozen in time, cars from the fifties still running, everything just slightly removed from the present.

It felt like a dreamlike, older South American town, as if time had stood still. Then, right in the center of it, there was this modern, white, geometrically designed museum. Omar or someone working with him had designed it, inspired by his geometric painting style. Omar's work was all abstract geometric forms, and he had achieved global success. He was also the favorite son of this town. And right there in the middle of it all was his museum.

On another trip, I returned to Colombia, shooting and preparing for the opening of this highway art exhibition. Omar was clearly one of the most important artists in Colombia at the time, aside from maybe Botero. His work was different, but he had cultural and political influence because of his international success.

In Omar's mind, this was about more than just art. His museum was in this town where he was from, and he wanted to elevate it. He wanted recognition for where he grew up. Creating another outdoor art project leading into the town was part of that vision. It was about turning this small place into a destination.

And it worked. The president of Colombia was en route to commemorate the opening. I was going to meet the president for the second time within a year.

Who was I?

How did this keep happening?

It was opening day, and I was shooting everything. The construction, the installation, the painting of the works, all of it. I had total access.

Then we heard it. A military helicopter overhead. It landed, and the president stepped out with members of his cabinet. Military officials, decorated uniforms, medals. There was a ceremony. Speeches. A moment for Omar. The press was everywhere, documenting everything. And there I was, this gringo from New York City, in the middle of it all. They thought I was some hotshot American photographer. Even at that age, with very little under my belt, I was developing this confidence, this personality that made people believe in me.

So I photographed the president, the ceremony, everything. And I asked, through my interpreter, if I could go up in the helicopter and shoot the road from the air. I told them it would be a powerful photograph. They considered and then said yes, but only one pass. They were in a hurry. After that, they'd drop me at a nearby military base.

I didn't hesitate. I jumped at it. This was a glimpse of what would become my future. Being confident enough to talk my way into almost anything. There I was, this young American kid, long hair, scruffy beard, climbing into a helicopter with the president of Colombia. They told me to go, and I went. We took off immediately. The side door was open. I leaned out and shot as we passed over the landscape.

Part of me was thinking: How was this happening?

But I was also full of adrenaline. Full of possibility. There was a sense of empowerment. A belief in my own ability. A desire to explore every opportunity in front of me. I didn't fully understand how I got there, but I knew something had opened. A door. A glimpse into a future I could feel but not yet define. We made one pass, and that was it. Fifteen minutes later, we landed at a military base and they dropped me off.

I got out. Soldiers walked me to the gate. The helicopter took off again, heading back to Bogotá, I assumed. And there I was. Alone. On the side of the road.

Cameras around my neck. Vest full of film, filters, lenses.

I hitchhiked my way back to Roldanillo before nightfall.

Pretty ballsy.

Back in New York City, Omar and I built a relationship. We stayed in touch and saw each other occasionally, often with my growing circle of South American artist friends. Through these relationships, opportunities started to open up.

After seeing my photographs of his town, Omar offered me an exhibition at the Rayo Museum in Roldanillo. As we discussed it, I realized I wanted to go back and continue photographing the people. I wanted the exhibition to be about them, about the town, seen through my eyes.

It was becoming clear that portraiture was my strength. I could connect with people, even without speaking the language. I could do it with my eyes, with my gestures. I was learning how to communicate. I was becoming a storyteller.

A couple of months later, I went back and spent two more weeks photographing the town. I reconnected with my young interpreter, about 16 or 17 years old, and we became close. He was fascinated by my American sensibility, and my New Jersey fearlessness. With no hesitation, I walked the town and photographed everyone. Priests, shopkeepers, housewives, the policía. . Everyone came to know me.

With his help, I even went into a brothel and photographed prostitutes lying in bed together. It felt like another glimpse into my future. Years later, I would find myself photographing Brad Pitt in a brothel. I wanted to capture every kind of personality in that town.

At the same time, I was still a partier. It was the 1980s, and I was in Colombia. I asked my young friend if he could get me some cocaine. He came back with what looked like a tennis ball-sized rock. A solid sphere. It was good. I went back to my room and chipped away at it every day, keeping myself in a constant buzz in this hot, exotic place that felt so far from my life in New Jersey. It was unlike anything I had ever experienced, and I was fully immersed in it.

Over those two weeks, I shot maybe 150 rolls of film. I had canisters everywhere. I was preparing to head back to New York to edit everything for the exhibition.

But I started thinking: *Maybe I didn't have to leave the cocaine behind.* This was the eighties. I had a big sport coat with shoulder pads. And I had a very bad idea. I decided I would hide it in the shoulder pads and bring it back with me.

Don't even ask.

I spent nights, completely wired, opening the lining of the jacket thread by thread. I carefully packed what was left, maybe half of that original ball, into the padding using duct tape. Then I sewed the lining back up so perfectly you couldn't tell.

I was determined to make it flawless.

I flew back to JFK and went through customs. I was convinced that my two silver Halliburton cases, full of camera equipment and 150 rolls of film, would distract them. I asked for a hand check on the film, which made everything more complicated and more suspicious. They went through everything carefully. Then one of the officers pulled me aside.

"When you're done, step into that room."

I knew immediately. *I'm fucked.*

I walked into the room. They told me to take off my clothes. I did. They checked everything. Every seam, every hem, every inch of fabric, running it through their fingers.

They didn't find it. I don't know how. They were suspicious. Of my hair, my gear, my whole presence. But they didn't find it.

Maybe the universe was giving me a pass.

I got dressed, walked out into JFK, stepped into the sunlight, and got into a cab back to my apartment in the West Village. I had never felt fear like that. My mouth was dry for days. It was the stupidest thing I had ever done. I could have ended up in federal prison. For cocaine. How dumb is that?

But it *was* pretty good cocaine.

And yes, when I got home, I opened the jacket and did a line to celebrate.

A few weeks later, after processing the film and doing a tight edit, I planned my return to Roldanillo for the exhibition. I also landed an assignment from *GeoMundo*, a Spanish-language magazine, to photograph architecture in Bogotá. So I stopped there first. I spent a week walking the city, photographing everything. This was the height of cartel activity. It was dangerous. But I didn't think about it. I just walked around like I owned the place.

At one point, I was photographing the presidential palace in Plaza de Bolivar when a guard approached me.

"What are you doing?"

Then, "Come with us."

Here we go again.

They brought me inside. Told me to wait. And then, the president walked in.

He recognized me from before.

"I saw you from the window," he said. "What are you doing?"

I explained. He smiled.

"Would you like to photograph the inside of the palace?"

It was a huge opportunity. No one had really shot inside before, certainly not like this. And now I had full access. He gave me a tour himself.

I photographed everything. He introduced me to the cultural minister, who opened even more doors for me. It was surreal. I didn't speak the language. I had barely interacted with him before. But somehow, he remembered me. From there, I went to Roldanillo for the exhibition. Bobbi and my brother-in-law Dennis came down. We spent our days in cafes, walking the streets, waiting for the opening. I remember a teal Chevy from the 1950s driving through town with speakers on the roof, announcing my show. Like something out of The Blues Brothers.

"Señores y señoritas... esta noche en el Museo Rayo... fotografías de *Timoteo Blanco...*"

And everyone came.

They came to see themselves. Their faces were on the walls.

I gave a speech in Spanish, written with my interpreter. I told them that maybe, through my eyes, they could see themselves. That I wanted to show them the beauty I saw in their faces and in their town.

It was emotional. For them, and for me.

It felt like the beginning of something.

I was just out of college, but I was starting to understand my ability. My way of communicating. Not just with words, but with presence, with instinct, with the camera.

This led to more trips. More work. And eventually, I brought this body of work to *Rolling Stone*. After months of trying to get in, they finally said yes.

They saw something in it. Something different. And they gave me my first real assignment. It was a big moment. A turning point.

Because while I had proven I could do this kind of work, traveling, documenting, being scrappy, that wasn't the future I saw for myself.

I wanted music. I wanted celebrities. I wanted portraits of people the world knew.

And now, I was on my way.

Chapter 8
Rock Solid

In the mid-1980s, I became a regular photographer for *Rolling Stone* magazine, right at the apex of music and movies colliding in pop culture. The late nights of my youth watching classic black-and-white movies and listening to The Beatles was paying off in a major way. My first photo for RS was of singer Elvis Costello. This was a big moment for me. My first shoot for the magazine and for a big star of the moment. Then in 1988, Rolling Stone gave me a cover contract.

I started making a name for myself, and the money and status instantly changed my lifestyle. I was shooting music and Hollywood and doing advertising campaigns. I started buying expensive motorcycles and cars. I had to have a Porsche! Renting another space in the same Hell's Kitchen building, I turned the floor above my loft into a photo studio. I ran an extension cord from my home to the work loft. This was in the pre-cell phone days and allowed me to run back and forth between floors while living my playboy personal life and the life in my studio.

The work I was doing was exciting and included many magazine and album covers.

In the summer of 1988, I was hired by the band Bon Jovi to create the look for their *New Jersey* album cover. I was now considered an elite rock n' roll photographer and expected to bring my unique vision to each shoot. This shoot was a big deal for me, and I started scouting locations at the Jersey Shore. I rented an amusement park pier on the boardwalk in Seaside Heights by meeting the owner and talking him into my concept. We planned a big shoot, with motor homes, generators for the lighting, and many assistants. I hired the top makeup and hair people in the New York photography scene for the shoot, who were also my friends. I had everything ready to go.

But not everything went to plan. Bon Jovi called me the night before and said they wanted to use the makeup and hair people from a publicity shoot they had done the day before. I had to fire my friends for the shoot and bring on their preferred hair and makeup artist, not yet realizing I was about to hire my future wife.

Word got out about the shoot, and pretty soon Bon Jovi's album shoot location was blasted on the radio. On the day of, I got to the pier and saw hundreds of kids waiting for the band. Police had to lock arms and form a blockade so the band could get from their trailer to my set. It became this loud scene reminiscent of The Beatles' *A Hard Day's Night*. Once we were getting ready for the shoot, I met up with the new hair person and makeup artist Elicia Ho, who was a gorgeous woman and whose presence knocked me out. I had this amazing big photoshoot playing out in public with the hottest band of the year, yet I couldn't take my eyes off of Elicia. By another strange coincidence, Elicia who was just starting her career, had assisted Bobbi Brown doing makeup on the side to gain experience. At this point, I'd been single for a year and a half, and found myself falling in love with Elicia by the end of the shoot. The hairdresser on the shoot said it wasn't going to be easy for me to woo her since she was young and independent and wasn't going to fall all over me. My ego and I were up for the challenge.

A short time later on assignment for a Guns and Roses' first cover shoot for *Rolling Stone*, I asked Elicia to join me as the groomer. We did a 24-hour shoot in Asbury Park the day before the band was scheduled to perform. Elicia and I ended up getting to know each other better. The next day, I brought her to their concert and used my backstage pass to try to impress her. I was working hard to be her friend first, and hopefully more. She started to feel safe and happy around me. After months of friendship and work together, we finally shifted to having a more intimate relationship. I remember being upstairs in my loft in Hell's Kitchen and making out with her on my bed midday with a studio full of employees downstairs. I technically had an appointment with Julian Lennon that day, but I rudely made him wait downstairs because I wanted to enjoy this hot moment with Elicia. We worked often together and then became a couple, and she joined me on many of my travels around the world, including a *Rolling Stone* cover shoot with Bon Jovi again in London. It was there that Elicia and I truly fell in love with each other. A year and a half later, we got married, and would be for 20 years.

That same year, I bought one of the penthouses in my loft building and decided to live there while I kept the studio on a lower floor for work. That led to buying the second rooftop penthouse and living and working in them both. They were spectacular, with a large wraparound deck, gigantic skylights, and panoramic views. I kept moving through my career like a maniac, traveling back and forth to LA multiple times a month and elsewhere around the world for photo opportunities. On my travels I came up with a plan to meld the two penthouses into a fantastic home and find another spot for my studio. I renovated the two rooftop condos and created an amazing 5,000 square foot penthouse. My career was growing in value and so were my tastes. When I returned to New York, I decided to buy a building down the block from my original studio for a million dollars, which at the time felt like a fortune. I then started a huge renovation project on that building which I turned into a three-story rental studio/party space for other photographers, as well as a home for my thriving business. My NYC real estate footprint was growing, and even helping to change the neighborhood. I later sold that building and bought a five-story carriage house on W. 54th St. I then renovated that into a glorious studio that *Architectural Digest* featured in their magazine. There was a garage that housed some of my eclectic collection of classic cars and motorcycles like my 1969 Aston Martin, 1962 Corvette, my '71 Harley and '76 Triumph...all in NYC! The space was filled with my meticulously selected custom furniture, lighting fixtures and flooring. Around the same time, I also bought a house in the Hamptons. I was living life at the highest level, all on my own terms, as usual. At the time, everything seemed to be going so well, and Elicia and I felt like a rock-solid couple. My family always seemed to be there too. My parents, sisters, and their families lived in New Jersey, and my fanciful life seemed to be at its peak on a high from New York to New Jersey to Los Angeles.

Chapter 9

The Keeper of the Flame

Around 1990, still relatively early on in my career, I started working for a magazine by the name of *Parade*. This publication was a Sunday supplement magazine, meaning it was inserted into newspapers nationally in their weekly special editions. *Parade* was syndicated in many cities' Sunday newspapers and reached about 40 million people. In fact, more people read the newspaper than most daily papers. In particular, readers loved this supplement because it was a color magazine with lots of interesting stories, celebrity interviews, and visuals that they couldn't get anywhere else at the time.

In any case, since *Parade* was so widely circulated, many celebrities and people looking to promote their movies or special projects would actually get more traction with *Parade* as opposed to the more visible, higher end publications, which had a limited audience. Middle America wasn't reading these prestige publications every week like they were reading *Parade*.

Consequently, it was a magazine that I was trying to work for and get assignments. The *Parade* editors were always looking for great photographers so they could capture subjects for stand-alone pieces or journalist-written articles to make each piece one-of-a-kind.

One day, I got a call from the photo editor of *Parade* asking if I would photograph a gentleman whose job it was to protect the flame on the Statue of Liberty: Charlie DeLeo. The article, written by Christopher Phillips, profiled this Vietnam veteran and recipient of the Purple Heart with the specific job of making sure the gilded flame on top of the statue was always clean, bright, and had a fresh coat of gilded paint and that the lights were always working and shining on it.

While the United States Parks Department originally hired Charlie as a maintenance worker in 1972, the task of scaling Lady Liberty's 151-foot iron skeleton was not what they had in mind. In 1957, when Charlie was a fourth grader at P.S. 42 in Lower Manhattan, he visited Liberty Island on a class trip and fell in love with her.

After he returned from the war in 1968, Charlie's first order of business was visiting "The Lady". Then, he was hired to maintain the statue itself and keep the flame looking its best. He took his role seriously and, as my editor told me, was a unique character.

My editor suggested I call him and make arrangements for the photoshoot. Not knowing what to expect, I gave this guy a call and ended up having an enthusiastic conversation. He was really into the shoot and had this idea of me photographing him standing on top of the flame of the torch in the hand of the Statue of Liberty. If we made this arrangement for me to come photograph him by helicopter, he said, he'd make sure he was standing on the flame.

At first, I wasn't quite sure what to make of our initial conversation. I couldn't tell if he was putting me on or was even a bit crazy. Yet as someone who likes fast, adventurous toys, from motorcycles, fast cars and small airplanes, to helicopters, I jumped at the opportunity. Also as someone who lived for adventure itself, I was fascinated by how we were going to pull this off. Charlie told me that if he asked his superiors if he could do this photoshoot, they would probably say no, but he had another idea: He would spend the night at Liberty Island by sneakily staying behind as the last boat of employees left the island for the night.

The plan evolved and, he said, if I got a helicopter at sunrise and flew to the Statue of Liberty, he would make it his business to be standing on top of the flame. He'd be waiting for us to get a spectacular picture of him precariously standing on top of the statue, doing what he does every day, before anyone even saw us. Then, he'd wave us away as he saw the first boat coming to the island with the other Liberty employees ready to start their day.

Then, after I returned in the helicopter to the airport in New Jersey, I would drive back into New York City around 9 a.m. and take the first passenger boat to the island, so he could bring me up to the top of the statue and do the photoshoot his superiors would approve of.

Now, that sounded outrageous.

And it was right up my alley.

This was an amazing plan.

I called Teterboro Airport, a private airport not far from New York City in Teterboro, New Jersey, and found a helicopter company that would allow me to hire them, and we could proceed to plan the shoot. The idea was that I would take the door off the helicopter – a common thing when shooting photos from this vantage point – so I could hang out to get the best clear images. We would get there before dawn and then fly down the Hudson River to grab these pictures of Charlie standing on top of Lady Liberty's flame.

Around three or four in the morning, my crew and I headed out to New Jersey. My assistants Russell and TC came prepared with multiple cameras, film, and whatever accessories we thought we could handle in a moving open aircraft. We got to the airport and met with the pilot. Then, the helicopter company took the door off the hinges. We proceeded to take off.

In the air, we crossed over the George Washington Bridge and started down the Hudson River right before sunrise. We were barreling straight down the river as the sky started to get brighter. With the door off its hinges, it was loud, but we had our headphones on, not knowing really what to expect and if Charlie was really going to be there or not. The wind whipped in my face as I scanned the cityscape from Jersey City to Manhattan, with the Hudson River in between. Small yellow lights from the buildings were the only illumination before dawn.

At about two-thirds of the way toward the Statue of Liberty, the pilot's voice came on in our headphones.

"Holy shit," he said.

As we all looked to see what was happening, Charlie was standing on top of the flame, waving the American flag. The tiny figure, standing precariously on a surface that was gilded and domed, not flat, was a mind-blowing image. I quickly got my act together and, as the sun began to rise, we did tiny, alternate, and concentric circles around the statue. I put my foot onto the pontoon outside of the helicopter. Russell was holding the back of my pants around my belt loop as I hung out and focused my camera on Charlie while TC was loading and reloading the film. At this point, we were probably a thousand feet from the statue, which we never would get to do today, but back before 9/11, and at that hour of daybreak on a summer morning, we could pretty much do what we wanted without anyone taking notice.

We continued to photograph Charlie for maybe 20 minutes or so. Although I was literally hanging by the seat of my pants, I still knew exactly what I was doing. I was ready when the light kept changing, from dark blue with the lights on in the statue's crown to the beautiful orange sunrise. I photographed in both black and white and color, my assistant handing me different cameras as I never let my eye drift from my subject. The World Trade Center was behind Charlie in my frame, as was its reflection in the river. Despite the precarious nature of hanging out of a moving machine in the air while focusing through a lens, I felt an enormous emotional high as I pushed the shutter to capture this awesome moment. Later I'd realize that I was creating iconic images of someone who would become known as "the keeper of the flame."

When the first boat started coming over from Brooklyn, full of employees, Charlie waved us away. We ducked back into the helicopter and flew back to Teterboro.

Mission *almost* complete.

We drove back into the city and took the first public boat over to Liberty Island, as promised. We met Charlie in person for the first time, at least not from a thousand feet in the air. He was a small, humble man, so proud of his position that he radiated from the inside out. When we talked, he emphasized how he felt it was his job to make Lady Liberty shine every day. Charlie, the son of an immigrant, had created the job for himself, as he was first hired to change the lightbulbs in the torch. Since he started in 1972, he created a job for himself that went beyond the maintenance of an iconic landmark.

Charlie took me to the statue, and we went up into the crown, then through a small door to a steel ladder attached to her arm. We were hanging over the harbor, and you could feel her arm move and creak as we climbed up the ladder. The space was so tight that I had to keep my elbows in and my cameras tight to my chest.

We came to another little door at the top of the ladder, which swung open and I found myself standing on the torch of the Statue of Liberty, early in the beautiful summer morning overlooking Lower Manhattan. The position was so majestic, albeit a bit unnerving, as I knew I was doing something that no one had ever done before. Charlie posed for me, standing out on the torch with Manhattan in the background, a very proud man showing the country and the world his prideful position of protecting Lady Liberty.

That day, I took amazing photographs and had an even more amazing experience that would stand out in my mind forever. When the magazine article came out, the title emblazoned on the cover of *Parade* was "The Keeper of the Flame," with my photo of Charlie proudly standing on the actual flame, one hand resting on his bent leg. The photo quickly became a widely recognized image, and it gave Charlie a piece of fame no one could have anticipated. Charlie became known all over the world. As each new visitor came to the statue, people would ask to meet "The Keeper," now a sort of ambassador to its glory.

Every year, Charlie would send me a Christmas card and thank me for that day. He lived by himself in a little basement apartment in Brooklyn, seemingly a lonely man, but he was proud of his service and proud of his job. He was grateful for what *Parade* and I had done in bringing attention to his mission. He would go on to write his own memoir, *Keeper of the Flame*.

For me personally, Charlie had given me something that I felt thankful for: I had a newfound appreciation for not only his position, but for Lady Liberty herself. The experience made me better appreciate how my mother's parents both came over Ellis Island. The first sight they most likely saw was Lady Liberty. Both of them had immigrated from a small town outside of Naples, Italy in 1900. My grandfather, John Coppola, became a US citizen in 1920.

Charlie, this tender man with one goal each day, had made us remember how he was not only keeping Lady Liberty shining physically, but metaphorically providing hope for future generations who saw America as the land of opportunity. Similarly, I too was a product of my grandparents' hopes and dreams.

Charlie retired in 1999 when he could no longer climb the Statue of Liberty due to his age. Yet true to Charlie's nature, his retirement only lasted two months. He missed his Lady too much. He asked to come back as a volunteer, which he ended up doing on Ellis and Liberty Islands.

Twenty years after that article was published, I had Charlie come to my studio and photographed him holding a large print of that *Parade* cover story as The Keeper of the Flame.

Now, almost 40 years later, Charlie's contributions continue to endure, even garnering a mention during President Biden's presidential farewell speech. While I've since lost touch with Charlie and the most recent report of Charlie still kicking around is from 2020, he's always in my mind and a hero of sorts. To me, he will forever be a man on a mission and someone who created a name for himself by protecting something he believed in.

Chapter 10
Boys and Their Toys

When I was a little boy, I was fascinated with cars and everything car culture. It was the sixties, a time where both a youth movement was blossoming and everything to me was about California and surfing, music, cars, and motorcycles. Even younger as a little boy, cars were everything. I collected little Matchbox toy cars, which were the size of a...well a matchbox. They had every model and make, and they were made of a cast metal, but the wheels moved and the doors and hood opened. They were perfect little replicas of real cars. This was before Hot Wheels, which was more of a seventies thing. I guess these were kind of little old fashioned metal toys, but they were very detailed and really beautiful and I was so into collecting them. Whenever I went shopping with my dad, I always wanted a new car and I always spotted them in the toy store. Every once in a while, he'd splurge and buy me one. I'm sure they weren't cheap for him on his modest income. In any case, cars and trucks were something that I was always fascinated with.

As I got a little bit older, I started building plastic car models, which were a larger size, approximately 1/25 scale of a real car. I thought they were beautiful, and you could paint them and customize them any way you wanted. You used this really toxic glue that probably affected my young brain, but because you were assembling it, you could choose to not put all the parts on, alternate parts from other models, paint them how you wanted or whatever your little creative mind wanted to do. After building them, and imagining little racing, driving or crashing scenarios, I would sometimes set them on fire because they were plastic and they would burn brightly, melt, and produce a thick black smoke. Another possible source of brain damage. I would say that this was sort of the beginning of my pyromania stage in life. We'd also put firecrackers in them and blow them up. So it was all about cars and crashes and, I don't know, some sort of childhood aggression and violence I was living. I remember once setting up a miniature car crash scene behind a neighbor's garage that got out of hand and set the building on fire. Not the last time I'd get involved in some pyrotechnic mishap as a little boy, and that fascination had somehow become a big part of my life.

When I was 15, I bought a Volkswagen. Now in New Jersey, you couldn't get your driver's license until 17, but I bought the car anyway and used to park it around the block from my parents' house, so they wouldn't know. It was so simple to drive, and I drove everywhere with it. I remember I met a girl during that summer at the shore, and I had a huge crush on her. She lived up in Yonkers, New York, which wasn't that far, maybe 15 miles from my home in Fort Lee, NJ. After the summer I used to go visit her at home and heavily make out in her living room as much as we possibly could while sharing the house with her family. I had to drive across the George Washington Bridge, and then I had to go up the West Side Highway to the Sawmill Parkway, and then up to Yonkers. I remember the exit was Tuckahoe Road, and remembering the exit and navigating roads as this little kid driving a car illegally was a big deal. It took a lot of balls. I couldn't really pull up at her house because her parents, although they knew I was infatuated with their daughter and allowed me to visit, also knew that I wasn't old enough to drive, so I parked around the corner there too.

That was my first car. And then when I graduated college, I bought a 1959 Volkswagen that I thought was super cool. I believe it had a split window in the back. It was a piece of shit and I don't even think it ran, but I had this idea that I was going to fix it up and restore it. I bought the car in Boston after my college days in Rhode Island, and then I kept it on the street in front of my house for a bit. This was the beginning of something with cars for me and became an addiction that then carried forward in my life. I eventually towed it on the back of a U-Haul down to my parents' house in New Jersey when I moved from Boston to New

York and shoved it in the corner of my parents' garage so they could still fit their car in next to it. And there it sat for a few years.

A little bit later on when I was trying to build my career and take photographs of friends and bands and different things, I actually pulled the car out and set it on fire for a photo shoot. I called the Fort Lee Fire Department and asked them to participate in the shoot so that maybe they could practice firefighting. I remember taking it to a field that the fire department let me use. They showed up and they kind of used it as a test for their younger firefighters. I shoved old dried up Christmas trees into the interior of this Volkswagen so it would burn spectacularly. Then, I set it on fire and photographed this magician I knew in front of the car as if he had done something to make it explode into a fireball.

Now that I think back on that moment, it was the beginning of my talking people into things in order to get the shot. In this case, the Fort Lee Fire Department. Everything seems to repeat itself, as my memory of my dad and me running from the dinner table to follow the fire engines to fires, my fascination with cars that I was now using in my photos, even now setting them on fire like I used to do with my model toy cars.

As I began to make money and my career grew, I started to buy other cars that interested me. At first, it was a fast car for myself, a Porsche.

Then on top of that, I bought a 1939 Buick that I drove all over New York City. It was a beat-up old funky jalopy that was so much fun. Why do I like 'em like that? Because they remind me of old family photos, and of all the old film noir movies from the 30's and 40's I used to watch. There was something about the style of these older beat-up cars that captured me. I was beginning to not only have this fascination and addiction to collecting automobiles, but it was all tied together in some way to my interests and my history. As I got more and more successful, I started buying more and more cars. When I bought a place in Eastern Long Island out in the Hamptons, I rented a garage space, a warehouse, and started parking my collection there and spending every weekend driving them.

I met this really sweet guy named Larry Saccente, who was a local fireman, a mechanic, and sort of a dependable handyman. But boy did he know cars. He learned from his father and grandfather and was this brilliant mechanic who could fix anything. He became my caretaker of my house in Long Island and gave attention to all the things I had, but with a mechanical mind and the time to take care of all that needed fixing in my life. He could not only restore cars, but he could keep them all running. I kept them dusty, dirty, and beat up because I thought that was cool, but he could get them running and keep them running for me. I had quite a collection building and as one thing led to another, I had actually collected thirty cars at one time.

I was always buying and selling them. Like the Matchbox cars, it was more about the hunt and the buy rather than keeping them. And, it was an emotional thing for me. I enjoyed riding in them. It made me feel like I was Robert Mitchum in an old 1930s movie. There was something about driving around in these old cars in New York City or even out on the country roads in the Hamptons, where I felt like I was in a different world. It was some strange fantasy that connected me to everything: Cinema, the emotions I felt from the cars, and my childhood memories. It connected me to everything motor that so fascinated me and had my interest. And now I was able to afford it.

The more I started to buy and the more I built this collection; I started to drive around on the weekends and then started to photograph my cars. All week long I was involved in business, and my career of shooting people. But when I was in the Hamptons, I did nothing but drive my cars around and I went from one to the other all weekend long. I would start on a Friday night, and I would take one from the garage and bring it to my house. Then Saturday morning I'd bring it back to the garage, and then I would take a different one out and drive to lunch. Then I'd come back in the afternoon and take a different one out and then another one at night, and then I'd leave it at my house overnight, and then go back in the morning and switch to another one. On any given weekend, I might drive four or five cars, exercise and move them around, and then I would determine what needed to be done with them during the week.

Larry would work on the cars, and I'd repeat it the next weekend. It was a wonderful cycle, and all of a sudden, I was building this involved hobby. Now, I wasn't Ralph Lauren or any other big car collector. I certainly didn't have *that* kind of money. But jalopies were not expensive. Larry was also not expensive, but collectively it was an expense that I allowed myself as a relief during this stressful time in my life. I paid Larry under the table which helped him lead a decent local life in the Hamptons, but it also allowed me to keep my cars running and to work with someone I trusted. We kind of relied on each other. I could trust him to take care of my cars and my house, and he could trust me to keep him and his bills paid. It worked out for us both.

I continued to drive around on weekends, and as I drove around, I started to photograph the cars and look at this opportunity to create a unique body of work. I saw it as the "art of the automobile". Because I was photographing people all the time, I decided to photograph my cars without people. Why? Because I liked on weekends not being "on" all the time as I was during the week, and also because I believed the cars themselves represented something that had its own personality. I took portraits of my cars. They represented some personal thing. They represented something that really hit home emotionally with me. I would use cars in my photo shoots with celebrities and portraits all the time. Why? Because they had great architecture. They were great props. They were shiny. They had structure. They represented a time and a place and a sense of something that was a great addition to, and a prop for my portraits with people. But on weekends when I was photographing my cars, it was just the cars alone, and I'd pull them into fields...or I'd pull them on the side of the road...or I'd go to car shows or parking lots to photograph them. Sometimes I'd find a car abandoned and sitting in a field and I'd take a picture of that.

This body of work represented all of my interests, my history, and my knowledge of automobiles that I gained from my personal experience and from reading everything I could get my hands on relating to cars. I was on planes so often with hours to kill, and all I did was bring automobile periodicals and such with me, always searching for the next buy, and the next car that I could afford. And when I saw pictures of it, it brought up those emotional feelings.

In regularly making these photographs, I created this big body of work that I still show and sell today. It's been exhibited in museums and in different galleries. It's actually a really wonderful body of work that I photographed with an antique Polaroid camera. Consequently, the photos have this vintage quality to them that is very unique, in a way very different from the way cars are photographed by other people.

During my weekends, I'd drive around, get stoned, bring my camera, and photograph my cars. I'd kept them all in this warehouse, but this started to become expensive because I had so many of them. So it wasn't just about the cost to buy, but the maintenance. Then of course, cars needed to be insured. They need to be inspected, and I felt that expense was silly. I never would do that. I always used to pay a guy on the side to have my cars inspected rather than have to go through the bureaucratic process of having cars inspected by the state Department of Motor Vehicles. I was always sort of pulling a fast one, if you will, by making it easy for myself and getting cars that probably weren't legally or safely capable of being on the road made legal.

But, I managed to keep them on the road through my little shenanigans.

As my collection grew, I really needed to do something because I was way too busy to deal with these little games I played to keep my cars legally on the road. So I looked up what it would take to become a New York State car dealer. The criteria for having that business was not really too involved. I needed to create a website, a domain name, a business name, and a corporation. I needed to have a place with the correct signage, and register it with the state of New York in order to sell cars. What this did for me, if I could make it work, was to get a dealer plate, which meant that I could put that plate on any one of my cars and drive it whenever I wanted legally, instead of having to register and insure each one.

Once I became a legitimate dealer, what was registered and insured was the "dealership" and I received a dealer plate. Every car that I put that plate on was legal for me to drive, and I didn't have to go through the process of individually registering or insuring them. This became my hobby hack. I kept the registrations open as I bought the cars so I could just turn around and sell them when I tired of them, and I was constantly buying and selling. It was a weird little scam, if you will, that I put together with the state of New York because I really wasn't fully acting as a car dealer, at least not publicly. But as far as the state was concerned, I had created a business out of it, and it kept me buying, selling, and driving any car that I wanted to drive.

The more I bought, the more space I needed. I kept building and collecting junk, and cars and car parts, and automobilia, and I put all into this warehouse in Long Island that I just played in every weekend. It was like my own private clubhouse. I rarely invited anyone there. I mostly just played by myself. Larry came and went as I asked him to keep me on the road and work on cars, and he would show me the work he did during the week and I'd show him what he needed to do the week after while I was gone.

During the week, I went back to my life on the road and in Hollywood shooting pictures, but this was my weekend hobby and my opportunity to give myself some peace and pleasure despite all the insanity of my growing business. The more I built up this clubhouse, the more fun it became for me and the weirder it became. I can't even describe it to you. I had a mannequin in the office wearing some weird Catholic vestment that I found at some yard sale. I had odd memorabilia from the sixties from car shows, and car parts, and hood ornaments, and license plates, and just odd junky things that were all related in some way to the car hobby and to the odd eccentricity of my jalopy collection.

As I mentioned earlier, my father and I used to chase fire engines, and I actually later had one in my collection. He was always supportive in some way of my crazy interests with trucks and cars and fire and all of the things that little boys get excited about. For some reason, I carried it into adulthood. When I was a little boy I remember when sidewalks were replaced for whatever reason, whether the city was doing some sewer work or whatever, whenever a new sidewalk was laid and it was fresh concrete, little boys always got into the concrete after the workers left while it was still soft and wrote their name or put their handprint in it.

Throughout my adult life, I remembered that in my old neighborhood there was this piece of sidewalk that I had christened with my name... Timmy White 1965 and with this little boy's handprint. That meant I was nine years old when I did it, and it was always in my head. I was like, how cool is that, that my name is immortalized in this piece of concrete in New Jersey? When I was in my late forties, my father in his seventies, I talked my father into my crazy idea to go and take this piece of sidewalk and make it part of my collection. Well, my name and handprint were only in the lower half of this four-by-four-foot piece of sidewalk, so I wasn't going to take the whole thing. But I wanted to somehow take half of it and take that piece with me. So I talked my father into going on this excursion.

Now, this is where it gets really wacky. We went to Home Depot and rented a concrete saw. A concrete saw is basically like a chainsaw, only the blade is a large spinning blade, not a chain. That blade can cut through concrete. It's not easy to do, and concrete's a very hard substance. So it really is a tedious, strenuous, time consuming, noisy, and very dusty process. I talked my father into doing this with me, and the two of us went to Home Depot and rented the saw, and we bought a batch of concrete mix. We went to my old neighborhood in Fort Lee, New Jersey and knocked on the door of the house the sidewalk was in front of, and whose piece of sidewalk I was about to take home. At this point I had long hair, was scruffy, and looked a little bit of a rock-and-roll type of guy, and with this older man behind me I knocked on the door and said, "Now, I know this is going to sound weird, but I used to live in this neighborhood, and when I was a little boy, I put my hand print on this piece of sidewalk, which is in front of your house, and I want to take it."

I told them that I really wanted this hunk of concrete as a souvenir, and so "I'm going to cut the piece of sidewalk out and replace it, so you don't have to worry about a thing. It's not going to affect you in any way. I'm just going to take this piece of sidewalk, and I will fix it and pour new cement when I'm done." And for some reason, I talked these people into it. They were like, okay, fine, as long as you replace it, it doesn't matter to us. I don't think they really thought about what we were doing.

I couldn't believe I could I talk people into doing nutty stuff with me. Not just my father to come along on this insanity, but these people to allow me to do this in front of their house. The fact that I didn't even think twice that the sidewalk was city property, or that there was probably a law, but also a process with which a city agency, maybe the Department of Public Works, or some independent contractor would be hired by the city who would be the people who made new sidewalks. But that didn't matter to me. Joe White and I needed to get this piece of sidewalk as part of the Tim White Memorabilia collection. We started to cut the concrete, my father crouched on the sidewalk with me. As we were cutting concrete, this cloud of dust started to form in the neighborhood, and it was covering the cars and the houses. At one point, we were engulfed in it and everything was covered in white dust.

It was hysterically funny. This big cloud of white dust was filling the whole block and in front of this house where we were destroying their sidewalk. But we managed to cut it. We lifted up this 300-pound hunk of concrete and put it in the back of my vehicle. I think I had a Jeep SUV at the time, and we put it on a dolly and put it into the back of this truck. We then poured concrete and smoothed it out and replaced the sidewalk and even put a little string with some sticks around it so no one would step in the concrete, although I guess it would've been perfect for another young kid in the neighborhood to come and put his initials in it. I never went back to that spot again. So maybe someone did.

I took this heavy thing with me into New York City and my father and I returned the saw. I brought back this 300-pound hunk of concrete with my name in it and my little baby handprint to my deck on my penthouse in New York City. And there it sat for many years until I moved to another building, a little further uptown, and I moved it with me then. I carried this piece of my history, this piece of who I was with me for many years, probably into my late fifties, so I probably carried around this piece of concrete for 10 years or more.

It wasn't until I got divorced, sold my properties in NYC and then moved to LA, that I then took everything from NYC, moved it all out to my warehouse in Long Island, where I stored everything until I could figure out what to do with it all. I still had the house in Long Island, and this warehouse full of cars and car parts, furniture. All the things from my life in New York City that I had since left behind, and had not moved to LA.

About six months later, I decided that both owning a house in the Hamptons and living in Los Angeles did not make a lot of sense. With my financial troubles and my newfound bachelorhood and a different life I had created on the West Coast, I decided to sell the home in Long Island and finally move out to LA permanently without this baggage.

Consequently, I needed to empty everything from inside my Long Island warehouse. My girlfriend at the time and I came out from Los Angeles one weekend and put notices all over Craigslist about a home garage sale. Over a 48-hour period, we managed to sell over every single thing that I owned, from furniture to cars, to motorcycle and car parts, to odds and ends, all of the shit that I had collected over the years. It was unbelievable that we actually cleaned out this warehouse of collected items over a period of a couple of decades and sold everything in two days. I'll never forget being in our hotel room in the Hamptons that night, just holding $20,000 in wads of cash. I was so excited to have cleansed this part of my life, and to have finally allowed myself to move into this next chapter, free and clear of all of the stuff that I had collected over the years.

The one thing we didn't sell, and I didn't get rid of, was this hunk of concrete with "Timmy White" in crude juvenile script and a boy's handprint.

Who would want it other than me?

It seemed silly, but that was what was left in the garage. On the final day before packing up and moving to California, Larry and I carried out this hunk of concrete and dumped it in the weeds on the side of the storage warehouse.

Years later, I checked with Larry who told me nothing had changed in that neighborhood and that my hunk of concrete with my handprint, name, and date were still sitting, stuck in the mud and the weeds in the Hamptons. I guess somehow leaving behind a piece of me there, and leaving behind a big piece of my past, but also leaving a memory of it behind for posterity.

Chapter 11
Amboy, My Kind of Town

During a motorcycle trip through the Mojave Desert with my assistant and his dad in 1998, we came upon this California ghost town in the Mojave Desert. Its name was Amboy and it may have been the dustiest, driest place I'd ever seen. It was really just a road stop in the middle of nowhere on Route 66. The town was just about dead, collapsed from the effort of trying to find something to do with itself. A good friend of mine and I decided to buy it.

I know it sounds a little crazy, but I get obsessed with things. Something about this ghost town really grabbed me; I had to have it.

It had a desolate small motel/café/gas station with a sign that read, "Entire town for sale." This place was perfect to me. The architecture was a quirky mix of 30's, 40's and 50's worn out structures, where the paint was peeling perfectly and the whole place felt like time had stopped. It was a movie set to me. After staying the day and spending the night, I decided to buy the town of Amboy, California, 1,000 acres, home to 11 people and located east of Ludlow, CA on Route 66 and about 50 miles from Twentynine Palms, the marine base. It seemed crazy to own a town, but to me, it was really just another one of my fun, out of the box, alternative ideas. My best friend and attorney Dan DiBenedetto, a judge in New Jersey and my party partner-in-crime, would always accommodate my whims. In this case, my phone call saying I found a town I wanted to buy, was no different. He said, "OK, we'll figure it out." So we bought it. We ran it as a location site mostly, for films and photo shoots. There was a population of 13: My friend Walt, who I partnered with on the deal, an old retired Mexican policeman who was our cook and housekeeper, and 11 other people who were still living in the town at the time. The truth is that no one really wanted to live out there. It was often 120 degrees in the summer months, and the traffic and visitors were almost at a standstill. It was really just some old buildings--some motel cabins and a gas station and a dirty cafe and a weathered old church. There were a few run-down homes where some of the remaining residents still lived and a post office that the government rented to accommodate anyone living within a 100-mile radius. I made myself the mayor.

After taking possession of the property and going back and forth on my motorcycle during my regular trips from New York to L.A., I traveled to Amboy for rest, play, and for photoshoots. I brought musicians and movie stars like Clint Black and Brad Pitt all the way out to my town to use the desolate location as my set. I eventually started having big parties in the desert town with my eclectic mix of friends, including Indian Larry, a gritty yet loving motorcycle shaman who helped change my life. He and some of my tough looking, tattooed friends mingled with celebrities, and other friends and family and we threw what would become legendary raging parties. Sort of my own "Burning Man."

I had a shoot coming up with Harrison Ford and I told him about this town I owned, and he laughed like crazy. He couldn't believe I bought a town. But I could also tell, just from how he was laughing, that he thought it's kind of cool. A lightbulb went off.

See, I had shot Harrison so many times by then that it was a challenge to get to something new, something different. As close friends, we'd bust on each other. While he was very collaborative and cooperative on every shoot, he'd pretend he didn't know it was happening. It was a verbal game that kept what could have felt like another job more interesting.

"So you know we're shooting next week?" I'd say.

"Oh God, not again," he'd say.

"Yeah, fine. So what do you think we should do?"

"Well, you know, let's just get together for an hour and you'll take some pictures and I'll get out of there."

"Right," I replied. "Forget it."

So this time I said to him, look, I have this town and we have an airstrip and I know you like to fly when you can. What about flying out to Amboy for the shoot? This way, I get you where I need you for the day, you get to fly, which is what you'd rather be doing more than anything, and by sunset you'll be heading home. He said okay. The groomer and my assistants left really early in the morning in a van because it was a three-and-a-half-hour drive from Los Angeles. I met Harrison at an airstrip in Santa Monica.

It was a gorgeous day and it took us something like half-hour to get to Amboy. We dropped in late in the morning and I was supercharged with all of these ideas. A guy I knew who lived out in Joshua Tree 70 miles away was bringing in his '48 Harley as a prop. And we had this ancient truck in town that I was going to use somewhere in one of the shots.

Then there were the motel cabins. Those things are funky. They probably hadn't been redecorated since the last time people stayed there, which was around 1969. Harrison thought those were really cool. I think it was the orange shag carpet that grabbed him. Or maybe the weird flower curtains, hard to tell. Either way, he ended up loving Amboy.

It's been said that Harrison has a habit of stiffening up in front of a still camera. That may be true, but he's never done that in front of my lens. Something worked from the first time we met. I think it may have been an unspoken unity between us. That's not to say that every shoot has been effortless. I have so many pictures of him giving me the finger that I keep threatening to print the Harrison Ford "Fuck You" calendar. But this day was certainly going to go down as one of the good ones. Maybe even the great ones.

There was nothing else for him to do here in Amboy except get into what we were doing, and nobody to distract him. It was Harrison Ford in a snappy suit in dusty old Amboy. We traipsed all over the place for six hours and took pictures everywhere. Things like him tilting his entire body at a bizarre angle over the crusty earth of the Salt Flats. Or him climbing on top of old train cars. Then he got an idea, and started running at full speed. His suit and jacket billowed like a sail around him, and I was flying after him, shooting frame after frame. I was trying to keep up with him to capture that energy, that freedom that I have never quite seen him display before, except maybe as Indiana Jones. To me, this was so wonderful because he was loose and so theatrical. So not Harrison. But that represented something else, a comfort level he felt with the people here. A trust that I wouldn't do anything to make him look foolish. This was the picture we came here to get. At the end of the day, we had burgers and coffee in the cafe. He shook hands with everyone. Then, we got on the airplane to fly back to Los Angeles.

The whole time we were flying, I was thinking about the first time I met Harrison and how he gave us (me and Russell Ward my longtime assistant) the sense that we made him comfortable. It was around 1988. Those early years were about a certain amount of balls. Chutzpah. We were a bunch of 30-year-old stoners going to shoot Harrison Ford at his house in Wyoming. I wasn't sure how that shoot would turn out, but I remember thinking when we met that we would get great shots, and it probably would be amazing to just hang out a little bit and get an idea of what this guy's deal was, because of course everyone had heard that Harrison Ford is tough. I mean like a real-life Indiana Jones, but maybe not even that charming. So we went to his place, got the pictures and bonded immediately. That was the start of it.

Now, certainly it was true that he was rather aloof and we had to have a professional attitude and credibility, but we weren't afraid of him. I think he sensed that. We just hung out, talked, walked in the woods and took some amazing photos.

About 13 years later, I was flying in Harrison's plane and he was giving me shit about something or other. He could be a real ball-buster. He'd walk into the room and the first thing he'd say is, "Your hair is thinning very nicely." Real guy stuff. I see the goofy side and the real side. Sometimes I'd be in New York City, and I'd get a phone call from Harrison asking if I wanted to go flying.

"Sounds great," I said.

"Okay, I'll pick you up at the West Side heliport in 15 minutes," he replied.

Or if I was in the middle of a shoot, I'd say, "Harrison, I'm in the middle of a shoot and I can't go right now!" He'll bust me for a while and then he'd say, "Okay, how about in two hours?"

And in two hours. I was out the door.

I mean, come on.

Indiana Jones was waiting.

Chapter 12
Grounded

My first flight with the beloved actor – and my close friend for so many years – Harrison Ford was a bumpy one. We had been pals for years at this point, but our relationship was about to take on new heights. One morning, we rode our motorcycles from our respective homes in Manhattan to Teterboro Airport in New Jersey. When we arrived, he shook hands with his new aviation instructor, a slim, ruddy, confident-looking man who clearly had been flying his whole life. The instructor led us over to a small three-wheeled plane called a Cessna, this model often referred to as a "tail-dragger" since its shape is tilted upwards, making the back of the plane sit lower and feel cramped for the passenger. That would be my seat on Harrison's very first self-manned flight.

Harrison scrunched into the pilot's seat while the instructor took the front passenger one. I stuffed myself into the back of the plane with my camera around my neck, game for anything but also wishing I had popped a few anti-nausea tablets ahead of time. Anyone who's taken driver's ed or driven in a car with someone new to driver's ed knows that it's going to be a rough ride, but having that experience in the air was even more so.

The instructor told Harrison to taxi down the runway and, after a few minutes, pull the throttle back. Since this was his first flight, Harrison did this in a jerking, rushed motion. My stomach lurched for the first time that day as we sped down the runway, making our not so gradual ascent. The small plane rumbled, shaking us all back and forth. The co-pilot/instructor's voice remained calm and steady even as I began to second guess my latest adventure. The airport's radio gave an "all clear" that we were ready to take off. I felt the wheels lift off the tarmac and began seeing only blue skies through each window to my left and right.

We flew around for a few minutes and landed back at the airport and prepared to do it all over again since that was how he was supposed to practice: Taking off and landing multiple times. This became a huge test of my internal fortitude. I distracted myself from my wobbly stomach by taking stills of the outside and of Harrison in the pilot's seat.

My nerves began to calm down as I did the one thing I never doubted in our friendship: Chronicling his life through my photos.

Harrison and I met on a shoot in 1988 in Jackson, Wyoming. My job was to take photos for a potential cover for *Parade* magazine. My assistants and I got to Jackson a day early before the shoot. We were in our hotel at the foot of Grand Teton National Park, a bevy of extraordinarily beautiful wildlife, clear lakes, and alpine terrain. The late afternoon light illuminated the orange and red leaves on the cottonwood trees along a pristine lake, with the awe-inspiring background of gray mountains, a living, breathing Bob Ross painting. I decided to call Harrison with the number I was given for his house and see if he wanted to take advantage of this beautiful end-of-the-day summer light and take some photos. Although the shoot wasn't scheduled until tomorrow, it would be a shame to waste this day.

"Harrison Ford, please," I said.

"This is him," he replied gruffly.

"Hey, this is Timothy White, the photographer from *Parade* magazine! I was just wondering, I'm here in town for tomorrow's shoot, but the light is so good now I thought we could get together and take some photos..."

Long pause. For a moment, I thought the phone went dead.

"Yeah, come on over," he finally said.

I jumped at the invitation. My assistants and I gathered the camera equipment and drove through a mosaic of late summer colors along the gravel road leading to the entrance of his ranch. Taking a deep breath, I knocked on the door, bracing myself for what he might say to me in person. When the door opened, he was dressed in a light blue denim button down, jeans, and sand-colored boots. His down-to-earth, every man's look belied the fact that he was the most desirable Hollywood actor of all time. He was also one of the most private men I've ever met.

He sized us all up: I had long hair and four days growth on my face. Initially, he had no idea what to expect, but it was clear that seeing these young, somewhat grungy guys seemed to make him feel more comfortable.

"The light's really great; I thought we could take some pictures...now," I said with an eager smile, hoping he was starting to like us but not sure he did just yet.

Waiting a few beats, Harrison nodded and began walking out of the doorway with his brown Labrador retriever, Ben, following close behind. I took him to an open field by the house and asked him to sit next to Ben. Just as I suspected, the warm light contrasting with his blue jeans and this beautiful dog made for a perfect portrait of man and best friend. I knew how to photograph him, as I was quickly becoming known as a "man's man" photographer in the business. He felt me, and I felt him, in that moment. Later, when I got the photos back, the picture was so detailed and sharp you could see his address/phone number embossed on Ben's dog tags. I took it upon myself to retouch them out of the final image, protecting his privacy.

As the shoot went on, I sporadically showed him Polaroid test shots. This process earned his trust, and he nodded his approval of the work I was doing. Our impromptu photoshoot was beginning to cement what was to become our over 30-year friendship.

Then, we took a walk through the woods and began to bond over shared interests: Motorcycles, cars, and, although neither of us had one at the time, airplanes.

"I think I'm going to start taking lessons," he said as we walked back to the log cabin along his gravel driveway. I nodded.

"I always wanted to try it," I said.

Back at the cabin, Harrison and I sat in two Adirondack chairs along with my two assistants, TC and Russell. We sat comfortably and talked for a while as the sun was going down. It was clear he and I, both busy in our respective careers, appreciated the space we were creating together.

"Are you married?" he asked.

"No, but I'm with someone I really like," I said, mentioning that I'd just met Elicia at the time. So much was happening with me that year, that I knew 1988 was going to be transitional for me. I'd just shot the new Bon Jovi album cover. I went to Iceland to shoot Bjork. Tom Cruise, Jeff Goldblum, Ziggy Marley, Ellen DeGeneres, Robert Mitchum (*my idol*), Hall & Oates, Ray Charles, Bill Murray, Joan Rivers, Keith Richards, Michael Caine, Michelle Phillips, Audrey Hepburn, Jay-Z, all photoshoots for magazines or album covers. I was blossoming from a young photographer to an established and even coveted one.

At the time, Harrison was married to Melissa Mathison, the writer of the movie *ET*. She was a lovely, intelligent woman. They had two handsome young kids and spent their summers on this beautiful ranch with the Snake River running right through the property. I showed up in the best year of my life and made an instant connection with Indiana Jones himself.

"So, what time do you want to start shooting tomorrow?" I asked, changing the subject.

Harrison looked at me like I was out of my mind.

"What are you talking about? We just did the shoot!"

"No, no that was extra," I said, smiling. "Tomorrow's the shoot day."

Another long pause from Harrison, leaving me on pins and needles.

"Alright," he finally said. "I'll give you the morning."

"OK, see you at 8 a.m. so we can get the early light."

My first photoshoot with Harrison led to many, many more. I shot him for the covers of many magazine and movie advertising posters and he, in turn, lauded me at different shared events. He also wrote the foreword to one of my books. It was a mutual admiration, but more than that, our friendship provided two different things that we both needed but didn't necessarily voice: I was looking to a mentor-type person for companionship and validation in my new fast-paced life, while he was looking for someone he could be a regular guy around, not Mr. Hollywood with the extreme private life that I believed could isolate him. I began to become a part of his family and kept his private life safe like any good friend would.

Our friendship, which would go on for the next thirty plus years, I believe was somehow grounding for him, something that also came from his new hobby: Flying airplanes.

Fast forward to 1998, I shot the movie poster for his movie *Six Days, Seven Nights* with his co-star, the late actor Anne Heche, in Hawaii. In that movie, he flew a De Havilland Canada DHC-2 Beaver made in the 1960s, a single-engine aircraft. It's called a "puddle jumper," as it could take off and land on very short runways. He fell in love with that plane and decided to buy one. The plane was restored to his precise requests. At this point, I'd flown with him for a while. I was collecting classic cars and motorcycles at the time, and now I had a front row seat to someone collecting classic planes. I got to be a part of something he knew I liked to share.

During the summer months when his kids were off from their school in NYC, Harrison wanted to have his flying machines with him in Wyoming. By this time, he had his own hangar at Teterboro Airport with eight planes and one helicopter. We had already migrated his planes out West so that he could fly all summer. But the helicopter needed to get there and Harrison came back east to fly the helicopter to his ranch and invited me along. We took off from the airport in New Jersey. It took us four days to fly and eventually land it in his backyard in Wyoming. Flying in this particular aircraft felt like an elevator with the cable being snapped and dropped intermittently while flying forward at 2,000 feet in the air. This wasn't the smooth ride of an airplane; it felt like I was being held aloft. At first, it felt a bit precarious. That took some getting used to, but we stopped a lot to rest and refuel which made it a bit easier.

With small airplanes, when you hit bad weather, you either fly through it or around it. At one point, a storm was obviously ahead, and having the advantage of landing a helicopter anywhere, we just landed in the middle of nowhere in the Black Hills of the Dakotas. We had to wait for the weather to pass over us, since it would have been difficult to fly through it. Halfway along our trip, we landed for the night in the windy city of Chicago.

After landing and tying down the helicopter to the tarmac, we went into town, checked into our hotel, and decided to go out to a blues club. Harrison and I were partiers, and each night across the country we let loose in different towns. From all my experience, this partying seemed to be a part of aviation culture.

At the club, we had a few drinks and listened to music. Many of the other drunk patrons began to recognize Harrison and came over to see us. Inebriated women and men practically fell across the table to meet Harrison. It was only a matter of time before he was bombarded by too many people, often asking for autographs.

"Do you wanna leave out the back entrance?" I asked, acting like a bodyguard.

At one point as we were fleeing, he murmured, "I get along fine by myself when you're not around, you know," he said.

Harrison didn't stop at flying small planes – he eventually got his instrument rating and was able to fly jets. He would fly himself around the world on publicity tours and family vacations. Life was imitating art when he played the president of the United States in *Air Force One*, and I couldn't help but think when he uttered the line, "Get off my plane!" that it was something he could have said in real life too. Maybe even to me.

My work with Harrison captured both the man in his natural habitat – whether he was in a plane, on a motorcycle, or in a natural setting working on his property – and Harrison the actor. For over 30 years, I was able to capture his life story one frame at a time. These pictures were deeply personal to Harrison and certainly to me. At one point, I took photos from one of our plane migration adventures and placed them in a leatherbound book as a gift. When I handed it to him, he was visibly touched; he kept the album on his coffee table and showed everyone who came over. I often saw it sitting there when I came over for family birthdays, holidays and get-togethers. To say that Harrison and I were family was real, as at that point we were woven into each other's lives.

Now comes the part of my friendship with Harrison that I've dreaded to tell. I was asked to have a front-page story done on me in the Style Section of *The New York Times*. This article would change everything. At the beginning of 2013, Harrison and I had been friends for so long at this point that nothing could break it, at least I thought. People in photography and the film industry knew of our relationship. But, at the moment I sat down for this interview, my life had been thrown into chaos. I was in the middle of a divorce, my aging parents needed my help, the economic crash changed my advertising business, and all of my real estate had left me with financial devastation. After all of that, I was moving from New York to Los Angeles. My goal then was to save face, to show people that I was still at the top of my game, and that my life wasn't crumbling around me.

When I sat down with the *New York Times* reporter, I was buzzing. It doesn't get any bigger than a full-page cover story in the Sunday Style section of the *Times*. Ready to show this reporter the breadth and excitement of my career, we started talking about how I was selling my carriage house to the Richard Avedon Foundation, a huge story that laid the backdrop for my seemingly perfect life as a big shot photographer. The story should have been the culmination of my career.

But for as much experience as I had working behind the scenes in so many scenarios with so many celebrities, I was a novice when it came to being the subject, myself. I wasn't prepped or trained for PR, as stars are. And as skilled as I was at drawing the personal out of a star, I didn't know how to see through a journalist's agenda. As the reporter began to ask his questions. I was trying to be natural and open, as I am, enthusiastically sharing slivers of my life as if I was talking with a close friend, rather than with instead of a journalist who was looking for a spin. and on the record. Looking back, I was being "flippantly truthful," something I didn't realize wouldn't translate to the printed page. I communicated with the trust that everyone would understand it, and with the trust that everyone would interpret it correctly, as if they were living in my world, on my train. Of course, I shouldn't have expected that anything I said may have been taken out of context.

The article was published on February 8, 2013, with the title, "Have Banter, Will Travel." Already, I was surprised and taken off guard by the chosen description of my profile. In the interview, I recounted my first meeting with Harrison Ford in Jackson Hole back in 1988, where I set the scene of the two of us becoming friends, and bonding while working together. My next mention of Harrison was quoted as, "Harrison's become a true friend...Truthfully, our relationship has really helped my career." That was it. No mention of our cross-country journeys, of our shared family gatherings, of my admiration of love for the man, and ultimately my appreciation for the trust he granted me which, yes, of course it helped my career, but that is not what our friendship was about. Out of context, this line on its own made it sound like I was only spending time with Harrison to further my career. Any other mention I made of him in the article was a non-issue, but conflated with this quote, it all suddenly became a huge issue.

The way I was misquoted and how the entirety of the loving, adoring stories I shared of a deep, real friendship were completely reduced to a sequence of words that were taken out of context was such an egregious stroke of journalistic manipulation. It made my whole heart sink while reading it. I didn't know what to do. What could I do? With such little PR experience I didn't know I needed to require a review of the article before publishing for accuracy. And now these distorted words were indelibly printed and degrading my treasured friendship.

It seemed that Harrison didn't like the article.

I felt desperate to explain and kept leaving messages for Harrison, who wasn't calling me back.

"What are you doing?" I asked. "Let's get together."

After multiple attempts, he finally picked up the phone.

"What are you, mad at me?" I asked.

"Yes," he said.

"Was it that thing in the *Times*?" I asked. I knew.

"Yes."

The quickness with which he answered felt devastating. I was used to his long pauses and then an answer, but when it came to this, he knew exactly how he felt and what he wanted to say.

"You know better than anyone that journalists take things out of context..." I said.

I was losing everything, and I was about to lose Harrison too.

Grounded used to be a word that meant something safe to me. That Harrison and I kept each other's feet firmly planted in a mutual friendship while we soared in the skies. Now, I was put on pause. Grounded, as in told to sit down, not to be talked to again.

I don't remember who hung up first. My head began to swirl, like I was in the throes of a full-blown romantic breakup, broken heart and all. I began to go through all of the stages of grief. Every day, I carried around the pain in my stomach, the shameful feeling that I'd destroyed one of my most cherished relationships with my words. The stability, the ground underneath me, was coming off the rails. The train had come off the tracks, and I had no one to confide in, as even Harrison had become a casualty of my crumbling life.

I even hand wrote a letter, *multiple drafts of one, actually*, and admitted that my breakup with him was almost as staggering to me as my breakup with my wife. True friends never break up. You're never left hanging. We had shared so many things together, how could it all end like this with some words taken completely out of context? How could he not believe in us more than what some reporter wrote? I sent the letter, yearning for a reply.

No response.

About 10 years later, at an exhibition of my photography at the Hotel Bel Air in Los Angeles that included one of my photos of Harrison, I saw a familiar person walk through the door. No, sadly not Harrison, but a mutual friend that I had known throughout our friendship. Immediately, it felt like an ex's family came into the room.

On one hand, I was elated to see them, and to have this memory of the past join me in the present. But on the other hand, after my excitement level and vibration toned down, we got to talk a little bit and a couple of things were brought up about how Harrison and I were no longer friends. and they shared their impression of what went down; that it was something that led him to not have anything to do with his past life. I was a casualty of this.

"Oh my God, you were family," they said.

Tears welled in my eyes.

My exhibition was such a bittersweet moment. There was a sad undertone to it all because it brought me back to the same feelings. And something deeper: In my family, we always stuck together. So, you had a bad day...you got it out of your system and we moved on. In my mind, we all have issues and things come up, yet communication is everything and friendship and family just talk and figure it out.

Another lesson that now seems clear to me, which seemed harder to accept: The realization that just because you feel a certain way about someone, doesn't mean they feel the same way about you. It doesn't mean you weren't in a relationship, but your feelings for them and what that relationship represented for you doesn't always mirror their own feelings.

If Harrison called me tomorrow, I'd pick up and hope to start where we left off. Because of the images I've taken of him, there is a version of time for me that has stood still. People come through your life and leave something that affects yours. Some more than others. My relationship with Harrison changed my direction and brought me a huge lifetime of experience. Until that time when we see each other again, I'm grateful for the over 30 years we spent together and for the flights of fancy, the mileage we covered, and the journey we shared.

Chapter 13
The Shitshow

The astrologer gently took my palm in his hand and began examining every line and fold. He slowly turned my wrist, looking to see how long my lifeline ran down the right side of my left hand. As he deciphered what the nooks and crannies meant in terms of my entire life, I looked around his darkened apartment. Heavy, velvet curtains fell behind this slight, gentle man. Then I peered into his face, trying to get a preview of whether my future was bright or grim. But his face was inscrutable. I sat back, realizing it was one of those moments where I couldn't take charge and make things happen. My friend Stephen Knoll, a hairdresser I had worked with on many shoots, knew a lot about what was going on in my life at the time, as most hairdressers do, and gifted me this reading as a Christmas present. Perhaps he was trying to tell me I needed to settle down and let the universe speak to me for once instead of me trying to be the one who always pulled the strings in my favor.

John, the astrologer, put down my hand. We weren't done yet. Then, he began looking over my numbers. He took out books and cards, all sorts of stuff. He finally looked up as if a bell rang at the end of a pop quiz.

Suddenly I felt like I was in a doctor's office about to receive news, as he was just as mysterious yet kind in the eyes as a good MD.

"Timothy," he said, pausing for a moment, "you're in for a shit show."

My eyes widened. Shit show?! What the fuck?! Are astrologers allowed to be that negative?

"What does that mean?!"

"Well," he said, taking another pause, "a whole lot of negative shit's gonna happen."

"But what does that mean?!"

He took a deep breath. "You're about to experience one serious change after another."

"For how long?!" I asked, trying to sound calm but faltering at the edges. I couldn't tell if I was nervous or offended that this astrologer thought a shit show was in my future.

"For a while," he said.

What the fuck, I go to an astrologer to tell me positive news like I was going to live forever and be rich. You don't come to an astrologer to get bad news!

I took an hour and a half out of my day for this?!

We finally finished, and I thanked him for his time. I walked outside into a brisk, fall day in New York City, and I was on to my next to-do, but the thought of what he said lingered. How was I going to prepare for one serious change after another? I still didn't know what that meant.

Soon, I'd find out that I should have taken him for his word.

In 2008, a few months after the reading, things started to happen. Family, business and my personal life were starting to get complex. The unraveling began with the unprecedented economic crash, which grounded my business to a halt. My once lucrative work in advertising photoshoots dried up overnight. Bills piled up on my desk. I was constantly on the phone trying to keep all of the plates spinning in the air. I was struggling to stay afloat and pay my employees, three mortgages and other expenses, which all totaled over $100K per month. That was a big nut to cover in the best of times for one guy with a camera, but with massive layoffs in Corporate America, it had been a matter of time before it came to my door.

The carnage was seemingly endless. I had to face employees I had worked with for over 20 years and tell them they no longer had a job. Hell, on top of everything, I learned one of my employees, my bookkeeper, had been stealing from me for years to the tune of millions of dollars. I was saddled with debt on my buildings in New York City and my home in the Hamptons. Sitting alone at my desk, the pressure felt like a garbage compactor on my shoulders.

Really, this was me now? John the astrologer knew early on what I could never face: I had gone from the cover boy whose Manhattan studio was a feature in *Architectural Digest* to holding the bag on high-end real estate. On top of that, my bank in New York that held my biggest mortgage and I ended up in court in a lawsuit that lasted for ten long years. It was all a continuing nightmare – and I still kept trying to work and travel and somehow keep everything running while it was collapsing all around me.

During one of those long days when I was on the phone trying to make deals with the bill collectors, talking to my attorneys, and taking any work that would drip in, I got the call. The call no one ever wants to get, and I was getting a lot of those lately. The one no child ever wants to receive.

"Timothy, Dad has been in a car accident," said Mary, my sister, sounding shaken.

Mary's husband was the president of the Meadowlands Racetrack, which my dad frequented, and got the news first. Apparently, my father was driving away from the track, had a cardiac "event" at the wheel, and crashed into a tractor trailer. Doctors couldn't confirm whether it was a heart attack, so they called it an "event." "Events" were supposed to be fun, like a concert, a gallery opening, a party, anything that I used to attend regularly. An "event," which caused my father to black out at the wheel of his car, was not a version I wanted to experience. He was 86 years old and fighting for his life in the ICU at Hackensack Hospital in New Jersey. Mary was with him, and I could tell by the sound of her voice that she needed me there too.

As I tried to piece together what the voice on the other end of the line was telling me, I realized I was still holding one of the crumpled bills scattered all over my desk, screaming LAST NOTICE on the upper right corner. I was still preparing and sending out employee severance packages. My whole life was crumbling, and yet I knew exactly what I had to do. I ran downstairs and hopped into my car and sped up the West Side Highway to the George Washington Bridge, back to my home state.

As I drove, memories of my father began to bubble up to the surface. Small ones, major ones, but one theme in particular. For most of my life, my dad was always driving in his car, and it was rarely for his own amusement. He was a good, hardworking man who spent most of his days acquiescing to the wants of my mother. While she was sleeping until 2 p.m. every day, my father was toiling at work from 7:00 in the morning and came back at 6:00 or 6:30 at night. By the time he got home, all he wanted to do was put up his feet in his recliner and watch TV after our daily family dinners during the week. On Saturday nights, my mother would appear in the doorway in one of her stylish dresses, and he'd immediately put the footrest down and drive her to wherever she demanded: Dinner and a show in the city, usually. He spent an inordinate amount of time in that car chauffeuring her around to her whims, even when he was dead tired.

"Dad, why are you always driving Mom around everywhere and doing what she wants you to do?" I said.

"The car goes," he replied, usually with a shrug.

The car goes.

The car goes, he would say to me.

Some of the rare times when he drove the car to someplace he wanted to be, he would go to the racetrack. While my mother slept into the afternoon until 2:00 p.m. most days, and he wasn't working, he drove the 15 minutes to the racetrack and bet on horses. He was such a dedicated provider for the family that this was his one sacred time to be, well, a little reckless. He continued going to the racetrack once or twice a week even after us kids left the nest and he retired. My mom would stay up late and then sleep later and later as she got older, and so he had more time to enjoy the track.

As a retiree, the car could finally go where my dad wanted.

And yet, seeking out his one guilty pleasure would be the scene of him blacking out and crashing his car. This was unfathomable to me. He was dad. The car goes. The car always went.

The car he was driving was new. It was one I had just bought him. But the car he depended on so much had stopped – and crashed.

Now, as I sped to the hospital to see my father in the ICU, my car was going. The car was going so fast in the direction of the hospital that it barely felt like I was driving at all. Truly the definition of what my father had used to explain transporting my mother all around town and beyond.

As I sprinted through the whooshing hospital doors, I barely remember asking where my dad's room was, but somehow, I was standing in the doorway. Mary looked up from her seat next to him, holding his hand. The sounds of whirling machines filled the silence. My dad, the one who always went, who always did for others, needed the help of machines to breathe. I could no longer ignore the fragility of life and mortality. A few moments later, the doctors came in to talk with Mary and me. He needed immediate quadruple bypass surgery. Due to his injuries, doctors couldn't do the surgery at that moment. We had 30 days to get him healthy enough for the procedure.

A couple of days later, my dad came to in the hospital. He had a swollen face, black eye and lacerations. I was there when his doctor came in to give him the news that he needed a quadruple bypass operation.

"What are my odds?" my dad asked.

"I can buy you five years," the doctor said.

Being a small-time gambler at the racetrack, he liked the odds and agreed to undergo the surgery.

The next day I went to go look at the car he was driving and to retrieve any of his things. I saw my father's blood all over the dashboard and the floor. It made me wince with a sense of vulnerability. For the first time in my fast-paced career, I had to take a step back. I had to help take care of my dad, weaving my time with him into my go-go-go life. As someone who felt so young and almost permanently 35 years old, I had to recognize that people did grow old. People did get sick. I needed to somehow honor the life I created, as well and be there for my father and family. Instead of running away to the next big great shoot or even dedicating all of my time to bailing out my own sinking boat. My dad needed me.

It was the least I could do for someone who put my needs ahead of his for decades – and I was often aware of my father's sacrifices, even when I was a somewhat "bratty" teenager.

When I was 12, on the cusp of being a full-blown adolescent boy, I wanted one thing for Christmas: A drum kit. Not just any drum kit – a Ludwig drum kit that Ringo from The Beatles played, as seen on their albums and countless photos of them playing music. Their iconic performance on Ed Sullivan changed the world, and that was the time I was introduced to the drummer Ringo Starr the icon. His drum kit with the small bass drum was, to me, the epitome of cool.

I liked to call myself a drummer, not a very good one, but I practiced and played into the next decade or so of my life. I started high school in 1970, which at the time was all about the music scene. Woodstock was just the year before. As a teenager, I experienced the renaissance of music in this country. That's where I saw myself. I had long hair, was socializing through the post hippie scene, using drugs, and wielding a cocky attitude. In effect, I was rock and roll even though I wasn't a very good musician. After high school, I wanted to go to college at the Berklee School of Music, but my parents talked me out of it, saying I could always play drums but that I needed a more well- rounded education.

In high school, I was in a band with Joe Imperato, *the only real musician in the group*, and the third member, Mary Ann "Tiny" Maisano. She was a heavy-set Italian chick who looked like she was in her forties... and she was only in high school. She played rhythm guitar in our band and had such a unique look. She wore a fringed vest and a cowboy hat and was very butch. We would do gigs at school dances. I was playing the drums and singing along with Tiny. The name of the band was Purgatory Blues Revival which sounds really stupid now...and we actually sucked. But my father, and my mother put up with us and the volume and let us play as loud as we wanted as we rehearsed in the basement of our house.

My father put in extra hours – on top of his already long schedule – to make sure I got a drum kit for Christmas. He took a keen interest in my request, and not only listened, but did the research to find and acquire what I desperately wanted.

On Christmas Day, my father led me into his office in our house and flicked on the light switch. At first sight, I gasped: Drums! I had my very own drum set! But as reality set in, I quickly realized those were not the drums on my Christmas list. The bass drum didn't look like Ringo's. They were a tarnished vintage jazz drum kit from the 40's or 50's. The Beatles wouldn't have touched these, I thought, and weren't at all in line with my own self-image as a youthful rock and roller.

Glancing at my dad, he looked so excited for me, and proud that he could afford to give his son the gift he had been asking for all year for the holiday season. I couldn't break his heart, even if my Christmas gift wasn't exactly what I wanted. Even as a bratty pre-teen, I knew better than to tell him these weren't acceptable to the level of cool I was going for. He was doing the best he could. With my dad, there was this appreciation I had for him even in those moments of my youth, and taking things in life for granted. Because my father was such a good man, I recognized that his intentions were always good. I'd learn as the years went on that my dad was much cooler than I ever thought he was, or than I could really ever be.

This gift was an act of unconditional love, even when the receiver was less than grateful or, at best, negligent to the amount of effort put into appeasing me with his effort.

Now, it was my turn to give back to my father. Even if it was imperfect. Being there was more important than perfection.

The doctor said we had thirty days to get Dad healthy enough for his life saving bypass heart surgery.

But what I didn't know is there was still a one hundred percent chance of a shit storm still brewing for me. Another serious change was about to follow with yet another transition in my own life.

* * *

Something came over me standing there thinking of losing my dad. After getting home, I went out on my deck and let out a primal scream into the Manhattan night.

We had 30 days to get dad strong for this surgery. This is where I started coming back into the family fold after being into my own life for many years. My dad had to survive. I had to help. My new mission in life was to get him well enough so that eventually, my dad gained enough strength and had the surgery.

All of a sudden, I was faced with having to help take care of my parents, while I was really having trouble taking care of myself. Suddenly, the glaze over the wonderful life I'd been leading was giving way to a stark new reality. So much of my wonderful life had evolved, but then the beginnings of the collapse of my marriage, my business, real estate, relationships, and my parents' life as I knew it, changed my reality. Everything felt completely out of my control. The world around me was forcing every cell in my body to shift into a different gear and look out into a road of unknowns. But alongside the panic was a kind of clarity unfolding.

Even later when I packed up my entire life and moved to LA for a fresh start, *and to open a West Coast branch of the gallery I partnered with in New York City*, I flew to New Jersey once a month to be with my parents who had now been living with my sister. Every month when I flew east and visited with my family, I would photograph my parents. Their aging became exponential and I felt the need to document it. I would take my mom out for rides, to a park, or to the cemetery to visit her family, or to the supermarket and make comical videos with her. My dad was more homebound with dementia, but I would cut his hair and dress him in fun dapper outfits which made him refer to me as his valet. I did these things for both of them so that their lives did not become stagnant. And I photographed it all.

I felt the need to share in this part of their lives and to have my camera be the witness. There was a feeling I had that made me want to be a part of their aging experience. I quickly realized the perspective on life that it was giving me. I also started to see them in a new light. It forced me to reflect on my youth and how they shaped me to be who I am.

I wanted to do something special for my father, like he had done with the drums when I was 12, and all the other times he put us before himself.

There is one moment in my life, a memory that always brings on such an emotional response. Bruce "Chaps" Boyle, a chaplain in the Navy for 34 years, and his commanding officer of an aircraft carrier who both rode motorcycles and who happened to be stationed in New York City for Fleet Week, wrote to the Brooklyn-based motorcycle shop once owned by my dear friend Indian Larry, the iconic motorcycle builder and rider who passed away in 2004. In the letter, they invited the shop's motorcycle builders, who were also my friends, to bring over their bikes to the ship and show them off to the other interested sailors on board. My friends asked me if I wanted to join, and I said of course. It wasn't until I got to the ship itself that I found out that this was my father's namesake ship during his naval service only some 50 years later. We rode our motorcycles to the pier where a few hundred young men and women from the ship were waiting. They had all come out to meet and greet my bike builder friends. Everyone was taking photos, ogling the machinery, and chatting with the builders. Since I was not a builder or from the shop, I stood on the side talking to Chaps.

"You know, my father fought in World War II, and in a weird coincidence...this was his ship."

"What?! The Wasp was the ship he was on in WWII? Is he still alive?" Chaps asked, to which I answered yes, feeling the weight of my answer.

"Well, this is kind of a big deal, because the Navy really honors its sailors and it's something that we take very seriously. If they've passed, we call them souls, if they're alive, they're survivors. Survivors are really important to us."

I told him that in another crazy twist, tomorrow was my dad's birthday. His whole face changed. "We ship out in the morning," he said. "If you can get your father here by 7 a.m., I would really like to meet him and show him around."

I immediately called my father and said I was going to pick him up from his home at 6 a.m. tomorrow and that I had a birthday surprise for him. Something about how this felt,a gift for him landed in my lap, was the kind of invisible thread that ties you to history in the most mysterious of ways.

The following morning I picked him up in Jersey, at my old childhood home, and drove him to that pier in Manhattan. The crew took him on a tour of the ship. Although they were hustling to prepare to ship off soon, they gave him the utmost respect and reverence. As my father squeezed through passageways on the ship, reliving memories, and being introduced by his rank and getting a salute and attention by the sailors, I got to see something that I lived for my whole childhood: Trying to understand and get a sense of what he experienced in the world as a young man. The biggest excitement of his life was his time in the Navy. This had been his moment.

As we were leaving the ship, Chaps told me to stand back and let my father walk off the gangway by himself. As he did, I heard that whistle, a seaman's whistle. I turned around and all of these sailors were saluting my father. I'll never forget how he looked in the morning light: As the sailors were in the shadow of the towering bulk of the ship or backlit on and below deck, my dad was stepping into the sunlight. My eyes welled with tears. "Chaps" gave me something that day and gave my ninety-year-old father something major. He gave me something that I'll never, ever forget. I befriended Chaps after that day and regularly kept in touch. We met again frequently, and I flew him out to my home in California. We went on motorcycle rides together. I met him in different cities whenever our paths could cross. We became friends because that man gave me something no one had ever given me in my life. He gave me insight into a man that I revered. I respected him and his service in the same way he respected my father. When my father died, I called Chaps first. He flew to New Jersey to spend a week with me and my family. He made sure my father was buried with naval honors.

The impact of the moment was life changing and almost mystical. A repeated sensitivity to moments that happen felt spiritual and metaphysical. This kid from New Jersey, who had this great career, was just one little piece of all of these dots that are connected in some way into an even larger human experience. I began to more thoughtfully look back on my own life as a celebrity photographer traveling around the world. Yes, I owned a town for 10 years. Brad Pitt and I spent five days riding motorcycles through the desert. Harrison Ford and I flew planes together and forged a 30-year long friendship. I've been on hundreds of movie sets photographing the biggest stars in the world. I've lived a big life, moving from moment to moment while capturing them with my camera. I've lived it hard and fast both in my career and in my personal life. I've never looked back. Yet I never had the experience of witnessing my father in this way, and I didn't even have my camera with me. Seeing my father in a new light answered so many questions I had about him as a child. And shed light on more of the kind of man I aspire to be.

As the only boy in the family living with three powerful women, I saw my dad as a soft, gentle guy with a wonderfully strong and cheerful personality. He was a role model who taught by example. He was an only child, his parents died when he was a teenager and went on with life on his own. He married into my mother's big Italian family and never talked about much except his time in the Navy. In a sense, my father was living each moment after that and was deeply entwined with my mom's moment. We all were. I felt abandoned by my mother's narcissism.

Her anxiety issues made it challenging for us to be close. She was too caught up in herself to be there for me, her only baby boy. She would act out like a child, because it was always about her being the center of attention. This not only made me resent her for not paying attention to me, but set me up to take on some of her same qualities.

For most of my life, I verbally jousted with her because of this frustration. Through therapy and later in life self-awareness, I now see how and why it affected me. In the last 10 years of my father's life, and finally in my mother's, at 101 years old, I grew to have an appreciation for watching this full circle of life. The hurts of the past formed me. But I realized her issues weren't for me to analyze. It was more about making me a better me, to appreciate the beauty in my parents' last turn around the sun. I was able to document it as well. In turn, I became devoted to helping care for my mother, holding her hand, touching her face and telling her I loved her every time I visited home. These last 10 years gave me a new view, not only of life itself, but of the beauty, the rarity, the uniqueness of my own existence. I owe my parents a great deal for allowing me to gain this perspective.

In my reflections, I realized how much I learned from my mother to also make everything about me, like it was all about her, in my career and personal life. Given the way I had chosen to live my life, this was eye opening. Perhaps my mom's influence shaped this aspect of who I became and now recognize as an opportunity to explore. Perhaps it's why I was always left wanting in relationships and often in my own universe, unable to see how my partners or relationships may be viewing the trajectory of our shared life. Today, I've gained insight into a career built on photographing subjects who were often narcissists themselves, or at the very least deeply focused on their own fame with blinders on to everything else.

What I didn't realize is that my father was going to keep teaching me lessons until the end.

Chapter 14
A Perfect Storm

On our 20th wedding anniversary, I wrote a heartfelt letter to Elicia. It was a long one because, well, I didn't know how else to express how much she meant to me. I wasn't a big jewelry or flower kind of guy, and I hoped she would see my sincerity in each stroke of my pen. Without showing the whole letter, *which would be a full chapter*, here's a bit of what I wrote to her, words that came straight from my heart:

> *Very few people can make a marriage work. It takes a lot to live together and work together for the same goal.*
>
> *You probably don't feel the same as me but I think it's been easy. You've been the best partner I could imagine. You're always there for me with support, love, attention and dedication. I only wish I felt it was equal.*
>
> *In the next 20, we'll cross from the kids we think we are to the old folks we'll become. It's as exciting as it is scary. I'm glad I get to do it with you. Think of how cool we can be. Think of how eccentric and fun we can*

make this next stage of our life. Think of how special it is that we'll have each other. We've accomplished something that many people can only dream of. Let's take the next stage of our life and fulfill the rest of our dreams. We can do it, I know, because we've done it already.

Let's challenge ourselves to be the best we can be. Let's challenge ourselves to do it together. Let's make the rest of our lives with each other new and exciting. Let's challenge convention and the easy way and make it our own. Let's better ourselves and each other by being present and there for each other every day, the way we have been. And more. And more. And more love. And more support for each other. And more respect. And more helpful, conscious participation in each other's lives. I love you, Elicia. I always have. I always will. Thank you for giving me the best years of my life. Thank you for allowing me to share in yours. I'll never let you down.

A year later, I walked through the door after another hectic day of caring for my father. My sisters and I had finally gotten him back to a healthier place where he was stable enough to have heart surgery. I was still managing to set up a work travel schedule and find jobs where I could. It wasn't perfect. I was still drowning in bills, but at least I saw a glimmer of hope at the end of this shitshow tunnel the astrologer had first predicted. After driving bumper-to-bumper from New Jersey back to Manhattan, I was ready to settle into my relaxing evening routine; Elicia would pour us both a glass of wine. We'd talk about our days. She would serve a delicious weekday dinner, and then we'd watch some TV. Then we'd go to bed, sleeping naked in bed together, oftentimes spooning as we fell asleep.

As I set down my keys and wallet, I could hear the solemnity of Elicia's voice.

"Please come sit with me," she said. "We need to talk."

A little thrown off, I walked into the living room and sat on an ottoman across from her while she sat in our big leather lounge chair. We never talked to each other in such subtle tones. Nothing felt "sudden" or foreboding as this did. She was still soft, gentle as always, leaning forward. The difference was how resolute she seemed in her eyes. No one was going to change her mind about what she was about to say next.

"Timothy, I don't want this anymore, our marriage," she said. "I've lost my identity."

What?

I was incredulous. I felt like I was in Harrison's helicopter, bobbing up and down until the cable snapped and the bottom suddenly fell out. My heart leapt up to my throat, leaving me unable to say another word. The enormity of my life, pressing down on my shoulders, had never let up since the crash, both economic and my father's. This weight was different. I could ignore a late bill, dodge collectors on the phone or ask for forbearance. I could nurse my father back to health with the support and love of my sisters. But I didn't know what I could say or do to change Elicia's mind or show her I was willing to change.

But what would I change? What had I done wrong?

A small part of me wondered if this was the first time I was really listening. Perhaps, I couldn't hear anyone because my life was too loud; perhaps, I never heard her. Now, I was hearing her voice as if it was the first time. I had been on my own train, and I didn't see anything else except the journey I was taking. Once I had the momentum in my career and life, it seemed too hard to stop. However, it's hard to say that I wasn't aware of anyone else; all those years, I thought I was being gracious and including everyone.

I needed to analyze everything I had done thus far in our marriage, right from the beginning. *Where had the cracks formed that I didn't see? What were the tipping points I unknowingly crossed and certainly couldn't have realized when I was writing that 20th anniversary letter to her?*

Had she known then, on our anniversary, that this wasn't forever? Was she being polite about my letter and all the times before when I was so devoted to her? Did she not realize that, to me, she was a fairy tale princess with an incandescent inner beauty and a calm, spiritual side that I adored? For me, she was the angel on top of the tree, the reason to hang mistletoe.

At that moment, it felt like she had become the delicate glass ornament that fell and shattered on the ground. Something was broken, and I wasn't sure how I was going to fix it.

But had I even caused it?

My mind flipped back through all the visual memories of our life, as it always did in good and bad times. This time, the carousel of memories stopped on my wedding day. On a vacation in Negril, Jamaica, Elicia and I decided we wanted to be together forever. I had called her father from the beach, asking for his permission to marry his daughter. He said yes. She and I had already talked about it, and I had brought wedding bands in my suitcase, though without her knowing my plan. On the white sands of the beach, I got down on one knee and proposed. She said yes. We even found the "town yenta," a local woman who secured a person of some denomination (*I don't remember which one*), as well as access to a boarded-up church so we could have our ceremony there. She also arranged for the marriage license.

I remember our wedding attire so clearly: she, a white bathing suit and sarong; me, a white tank top and white slacks; both of us, barefoot.

These two kids, so madly in love, walked up to the spooky, boarded-up chapel on a beach in the tropics and, within its creaky walls, promised to spend their lives together. A hairdresser friend of mine and his boyfriend happened to be on the beach the day before and agreed to be our best man and bridesmaid. Then, the party began. I, of course, took snapshots of the wedding for the entire day. Before selfies were a thing, I managed to capture myself and our small wedding party and passed the camera around so that the event was covered – *of course, that's what I do.* Later, I put together a precious little wedding book for us, which, to this day, is the only set of photos that I still haven't digitized, as I do for every one of my thousands of photographs in my archive.

As we started our marriage, I was still climbing higher and higher in my career, and Elicia was not only along for the ride but supporting me the whole way. We both became immersed in my fast-paced days of shooting, real estate, and construction. This was a big life; I had a lot of people around me; I worked constantly and was on the road for many days out of the year. I had a collection of thirty cars that I played with in my free time during many weekends in the Hamptons. My wife was a part of everything we did, working on our house in New York, the studio, and in my crazy investment in the town of Amboy, CA.

Elicia was with me the entire time, decorating each of the spaces and bringing her beautiful energy and style. I put her on a pedestal, though I was always the ringleader of this circus. However, we weren't always surrounded by throngs of people; when we bought the house in the Hamptons, we fled the city every weekend, only the two of us, and enjoyed each other's company.

It felt like we were always together. Many people saw us as inseparable.

Nonetheless, there was room for me to not see something. I was out of the picture long enough, mentally and physically at times, to not see there was a distance building. She was starting to live an existence I was completely oblivious to.

After I sold my penthouse, we moved into the five-story building in Hell's Kitchen where I also now had my photography studio. I was running up and down to my big office upstairs, while my employees kept everything working on the floor below. Elicia was helping me run the business and was downstairs during the day with everyone else: my bookkeeper, my assistants, and the ever entering and exiting stream of people working on my projects. Elicia helped to manage it all. One time, my retoucher fell asleep at his computer, and she texted me upstairs: *Cliff fell asleep again. Can you come down?* I was so busy and just told her to wake him up! My staff, clients, and friends were always coming and going downstairs. Everyone talked, gossiped, and knew everything going on. One of those people was John Botte, a friend who became one of my photography assistants; he came with a major backstory.

John spent 10 years as an undercover narcotics cop, then went 10 years as a homicide cop. He reached the rank of Detective Second Grade. He also was a photographer. He saw the most horrible side of humanity, photographing his experiences throughout his career, including after the Twin Towers fell, in the pit on 9/11. After inhaling toxic debris during his time in the pit, John suffered severe lung damage, causing him to often wheeze and cough uncontrollably, which challenged his overall health and longevity. He would struggle with the chronic effects of this condition for the rest of his life. Everyone John met personally and professionally knew about his health conditions as the years went on.

Then, because of his deep understanding of narcotics and his inability to get the proper health care for something that the medical profession was unprepared for, he started creating his own unsubstantiated drug cocktails that he researched and worked out with his physician in order to keep himself alive. His health was very compromised, and because the first responders weren't medically or financially supported initially, he and many others were left to deal with their conditions. Shamefully, many were dying. He used to make his own mix of drugs and shoot them up into his system, trying to keep himself alive, and, impressively, he did. It was the most unique thing.

I thought he was interesting; I liked the rawness of knowing a homicide and narcotics cop and the experiences he lived through. He also photographed all of his homicides. He had this book that I thought was so interesting, though you might throw up if you looked at the photos inside. It was very real. He seemed to have difficult family and romantic relationships, which made sense because he was a lifer cop who experienced a lot of weird shit.

My friend, the photographer Jim Marshall, had introduced us to each other. I was intrigued when I met him and built a relationship with him as I had with the gangsters, dominatrixes, bikers, and other unique people I had in my life. Given his condition and his retirement from the job, John no longer worked and began spending more and more time at my studio and eventually went on my photography adventures.

Sometime in 2010, John, another photography assistant, Gus, and I were all preparing for a big shoot in Hollywood with Harrison Ford for the *Got Milk* campaign. As I dashed around making preparations and calls at my studio, I saw John having long conversations with Elicia. He leaned on one of the desks, sometimes on her desk, as they laughed and talked. I thought nothing of it, at the time.

My office, on the other hand, was quiet and private. I had phone calls to make, so I didn't always hear what was going on downstairs. When I reappeared, I'd buy lunch and dinner almost every day for everyone, including weed and drinks after work. I was bouncing off the walls, building a career; even through the downward trail of it, I was bouncing around.

All of these people in my working life were on my train. Their job was to perform. I imagined the lunch and dinner helped keep them on my train, greased the wheels. I didn't see it as I was paying people to stay on the train or take advantage, but I was definitely trying to keep their full attention. I needed more time than actually existed to get everything done; 24 hours in a day just wasn't enough in my world.

On March 10th, 2021, John, Gus, and I packed our bags and headed to Beverly Hills. We arrived at the Four Seasons Hotel in the evening. We all went downstairs for dinner, then off to bed before our shoot the next day on the beach in Malibu with Harrison. Throughout the night, I didn't realize that something was going on in another part of the hotel. Apparently, John was having an attack and was ordering silver buckets of ice from room service as he began to spike a 105-degree fever that he needed to abate.

The next morning, I was focused on getting downstairs to greet my art director at breakfast and then meet Harrison for the shoot. Gus called me from our room, his voice sounding urgent.

"Where are you?" I said. "We're waiting on you guys for breakfast."

"You gotta get back up here," he said to me on the phone.

What greeted me was something John may have seen during his career as a cop and first responder: John was slumped in the bathtub, filled to the brim with ice cubes, with three needles lodged in his chest. He was catatonic but could still speak.

"Should we call 911?" Gus said.

"NO!" said John. "They won't know what to do. They'll kill me."

John knew that the medics wouldn't know how to actually keep him alive, and it was John's special cocktails that were keeping him here on this earth.

"Punch me," said John in a low growl.

"What?!" Gus and I both exclaimed.

"Get me up! Get me up!" John sputtered. "Punch me in the back!"

Gus and I heaved John out of the tub to a standing position in front of the mirror. John could feel my hesitation.

"I said punch me in the back!" he desperately ordered.

I took a deep breath and walloped him in the back. Warm, hard blood globules spurted out of his mouth and coated the mirror – horror movie material. He coughed and started to wheeze, having regained his breath.

"Gus, this is crazy," I said in a stressed-out voice.

"Let's go!" said John.

I gave Gus a look. *Oh, shit.*

In the Escalade outside of the hotel, as we were loading up the vehicle, John appeared. He was like a fucking walking ghost. He'd shot himself up with whatever cocktail it took and was determined to make it to this shoot.

Off we went.

We actually made it through a successful shoot with Harrison and his dog posing on the beach, but the hours on the beach working took a toll on John. The air was foggy and damp, and he began to wheeze and cough as soon as the shoot was over.

"I have to go back to my room," John said.

Later that night, we were all supposed to go to a steakhouse in Beverly Hills to celebrate another great job with the art director and staff at the shoot.

Gus was upstairs in the hotel room getting ready while I was on the phone with the producers of the shoot...but then he called me with bad news.

"You need to come upstairs," he said grimly. "John collapsed again."

Bursting through the door, I saw John in bed, catatonic, holding a towel with blood all over it and a needle in his chest.

"I'm not going to make it to dinner," he said, blood oozing out of his nose.

On John's request, we called my travel agent to book him a red eye back to New York City that night so he could go to his pulmonologist in Staten Island first thing the next morning.

That way, Gus and I could still have our shoot wrap-up dinner, save face with the client, and we could get plans rolling for John and get him on the plane later that evening. Honestly, I felt a bit relieved he was wanting to head back to NYC early, but I still worried about my friend and the alarming situation we had been witnessing. He seemed to be stable, at least for the time being, and decided to get some rest.

My team and I were eating dinner with the client at the steakhouse when my cell phone rang again.

"Have you talked to John?" said Elicia, sounding concerned.

How did she know about John? I hadn't told her anything that happened.

"I was with him about an hour ago. No, I haven't," I said.

"I think you need to go back to the hotel and check on him," she said.

Gus and I politely excused ourselves by telling our client that John wasn't feeling well and ran out of the restaurant. When we rushed back upstairs to John's room at the hotel, he was looking worse. He still had needles sticking out of his chest and more blood dripping out of his nose. He had to go back to New York immediately, as he needed medical attention from his doctor, but I wasn't sure how he was going to make it – if he could make it at all. He needed help. Gus and I were going to get him to the airport. We rushed him to the terminal and walked him right up to security to make sure he got on the plane, checking in with my travel agent and making sure a car would be waiting for him at JFK so he could get right to his doctor in the morning. He was quiet as he walked through security, and I watched him stumble to his gate.

Afterward, we went back to our hotel and stayed another day or so in LA. I was contacted in the morning and knew he made it and got to his doctor in Staten Island.

From then on, I didn't know what was going on with John. We didn't hear from him for weeks.

However, I never understood why Elicia knew what was going on with John that night when I hadn't told her about it.

***

Back in the living room with Elicia, I wasn't thinking about that last adventure we all went on before everything started to change. I still couldn't believe Elicia wanted to leave our marriage; I couldn't make any connections as to why she would do this. That night, we went to sleep in our shared bed, back-to-back. I remember thinking that we could work it out, that maybe things would look differently in the morning.

...But they didn't.

I quickly realized this wasn't something I could charm my way out of.

I needed to address this differently.

No, I couldn't accept this, my insides said.

But on the outside, my response had to be calm acceptance. Her comments were practiced, out of character in a way. She usually wasn't this strong in terms of her ability to communicate. But she was pretty clear.

"I've lost my identity," she said. "This is *your* life, your career, your accolades, your real estate, your success."

"No!" I replied. "It was us. I couldn't have achieved what I had achieved alone. This was ours." We continued to live together. In the coming months, Elicia and I started seeing a couple's therapist who, after separate and joint meetings, told us she thought we had a 50/50 chance. I wasn't getting straight answers from Elicia, and this comment from the therapist devastated me because I still didn't understand what was really going on. I continued to work hard at trying to woo back my wife by taking the time to focus on our relationship and to try and find what it would take to get us back on a better path. I asked her questions like, "*Do you want to have a child...Do you want me to give up my career...Do you want to change it all?*" I don't think I ever got an honest response.

Elicia said she wanted to spend Christmas with her mother, packed a suitcase, and said she'd be back. I begged her to not see this as an opportunity to not come back; I begged her to continue to work with me on our relationship. She left me alone for the holidays with her cat and the fear and loneliness that made me question everything. I could only guess she must have held onto these feelings for months and that she was done emotionally, incapable of confrontation.

On New Year's Eve, she called me and said she wasn't coming back. I held back my true feelings of fright and abandonment and just told her I understood that she needed time and that I loved her.

"You'll be back for my birthday though on the 5th, right?" I asked.

That wasn't her plan. She was running, but I had an emotional hold of her strings, and I wouldn't totally let go, and she wouldn't cut them.

She finally agreed to come back for my birthday. I'll never forget picking her up at the airport and hearing her say she wasn't coming back to our home but that she was going to live with her brother for now.

For weeks, I tried, in my own way, to woo her back. I'd drive up to Harlem and pick her up at her brother's, go out to dinner and try so hard to be the right guy and do anything for her. I was trying so hard, and every night, it came down to me asking the same questions over and over again: "Tell me if you're in love with someone else."

She wouldn't say anything in response.

"Have you just fallen out of love with me?"

Nothing – the silence was devastating.

This went on for weeks, if not months. I can't remember. It was so difficult for me, never getting what felt like a real answer or the truth, yet it was clear that our marriage had become lost, dead, instead of the living, breathing, ever-changing organism it once was. I continued to have hope and lived by myself in the home we had built while trying my hardest to believe we could resurrect the one thing I truly believed in and relied on.

Then one day, as I was getting ready to leave town for a charity motorcycle trip on the West Coast, she called me on my cell and said, "I never want to see or speak with you again."

We never have.

That was the end. I gave up.

My lawyer, and close friends, didn't understand. Everyone around us didn't understand. Her behavior was not who we thought she was. *Was she having a nervous breakdown?* I came back from my trip, and the cat and just a few of her things were gone. She left our life with nothing but a suitcase. Over 20 years of a life was left behind.

She just wanted to start her own life, on her own terms.

At least, that's what I thought.

We both moved on. Out of self-protection, I gathered myself with acceptance and dealt with the blow of my life and all the responsibilities left to me, including my financial problems, and moved on. After a year or so, our lawyers got together and mediated a divorce settlement. No conversation, no interaction. We both moved on.

Five years later, after moving to Los Angeles, I went to New York for my mother's 90th birthday. I was on the beach in South Jersey with my sister, Mary. I was talking with her about a 9/11 photographer I knew. I went on and on about this photographer who was so brilliant and that I had worked with, and was my friend, but we had lost touch. I was just saying the most glowing things about him; I remember that. I left the next day.

Two weeks later, Mary called.

"I need to talk to you about something," she said. "I've been holding it in for the last two weeks because I thought you may have known. After our conversation, I looked up John because I was interested in his work, as you suggested, and that's when I realized that you didn't know what I'm about to tell you because of the way you were talking about him. Apparently, he and Elicia are together. They're married."

I needed a new term for the bottom falling out of my life.

"What?!"

"Tim, I thought you knew," she said, sounding apologetic. "I was shocked, but I assumed you knew. I mean he put out a whole book with photos of her in it. How could you not know? That's why I was surprised you were talking about him like that."

My friend – whom I had included in my life, whom I had many experiences with, including trying to save his life that time in LA when he was having an attack – had run off with my wife. And I had no idea about it. Yet, somehow, everyone else did.

Five years had gone by, and I had moved on with my life with no knowledge or understanding or closure of what had taken place in our relationship.

The memories of that *Got Milk* campaign came flooding back.

"You need to check on John," Elicia had said.

How did she know he needed checking?!

I remembered their long conversations at her desk while I kept everything spinning upstairs.

I took the pain and put it in my back pocket because I had other things to do. Plus, I had moved on. I had put it aside out of self-preservation.

Yet there was a reason she had left. I just hadn't put it together. Elicia may have felt isolated as my career was in high gear, felt that she couldn't be as creative and free as she wanted. I thought she had it all. She decorated all of the properties we bought and owned; she went to the parties, wore expensive clothes, and worked at whatever creative jobs or projects that interested her. She had the life everyone wanted. Regardless, she left with a suitcase to go be with this guy who was always almost dying with nothing to give except, I suppose, a listening ear. He represented something that got her out.

Were they fucking behind my back? Did she go to his house from the home we shared together? Clearly, their friendship had become something else. Here I felt I was sacrificing my career for a friend of mine to care for his health and get him through this period in his life with no job and serious health issues, and now I look back and wonder, "What the fuck was going on there?" *Who knew anything here? Was I being laughed at? Did all my friends know?*

I started to get all of this anxiety. *Why was I getting anxiety?* I finally asked myself. They moved on a long time ago, and so did I. *This was five years ago, so why was I feeling this? Had I been pushing all of these feelings down?*

Maybe.

I decided to push it all down again.

Add it to the list, add it to the weight on my shoulders: my lawsuit with the bank for millions of dollars that seemed to never end; my parents' aging needs; debt and notes to the tune of millions of dollars. Then Elicia left me. All of this, the enormity of all of this, felt like it was driving me into the ground. That reading with the astrologist had to mean something because here was the shitshow.

Perhaps, the downsides of my life allowed Elicia to go look elsewhere for support. With all the negative things that I represented in the relationship, that anyone in a relationship has, built up, and on top of it, I had financial problems; I had parental problems; my time was always occupied with me – she was probably thinking, "I'm 40-something. What did I buy into here?" The truth of the matter was, I had considered all of that and saw that we had a great situation. I thought I didn't demand a lot, I wasn't absent, but I was.

I guess this was enough, in any case, that it may have given her pause to go and look elsewhere for something. What came in was this guy who didn't have anything going on, no work, bad health, and lots of baggage, and yet, he was able to give her the attention that she needed. I'll never know the truth.

But again, I shoved it all down.

I wouldn't let it sink in.

Stay in motion – that's all I did. Like jumping on random lily pads, I kept up with the current of the water and continued on to find solid ground.

This way of living through the grief of my marriage could only take me so far.

Eventually, the emotional limbo would all catch up to me...

...And show itself in my relationships to come.

Chapter 15

Eating with Aretha

Aretha Franklin walked out of her house wearing skin-tight, black bicycle shorts, put on a bike helmet and straddled her bicycle – a cutesy little girl's kind of bike, really, with a plastic flower basket on the front. She stared at me, signaling that she was ready. She wanted me to take her picture in this outfit. There was no way we were going to use this picture – ever, anywhere. *But what do you say to Aretha, especially when she's dressed in a get-up like that?*

This was the end of a long day of shooting for an album cover that started quite a few hours earlier. We had been at the Fox Theater in Detroit, this gorgeous old place where Aretha wanted to be photographed. About three-quarters of the way through the shoot, she decided she wanted us to go back to her house. We had other locations set up around the theater, but she'd had enough of this. But first, there was lunch, soul food – ribs, corn bread, black eyed peas. She had told us what she wanted and where she wanted it from, and we'd had it catered.

We all ate lunch, and then my assistants started packing up so we could race over to her house. Suddenly, Aretha was pissed off. We'd all eaten this huge lunch, and the caterers had packed up the food and left. And she said, "I wanted more. What happened to all that food?" So she called the caterers and had them do it all over and, this time, bring it to her house...and I'm talking a whole other meal, two hours later. The whole thing *repeated*.

Finally, we were in her yard, setting up, playing around with lights, figuring out how to get some great pictures. Some time went by, and I heard the house door slam. There she was, in stretchy, black, Lycra bike shorts, some sort of little top and a fucking helmet. I had a long lens on my camera, and I pulled back to see what all of this looked like through the lens. I couldn't believe what I was seeing. She was just standing there, looking at me, and I turned to the art director like, *Do you believe what we're looking at?* I considered the situation. I took a Polaroid to check the lights, and suddenly it hit me. As absurd as it was at the time – and it was absurd – I thought, "What will it feel like to come across this picture of Aretha 20 years from now? I mean, it's Aretha, for Christ's sake."

I took the picture.

That particular session with Aretha had started off very, very differently, and the fact that we ended up shooting her in bike shorts in her backyard was further proof of my philosophy that you'd better have a good bag of tricks ready because you never know what crazy twists and turns a day can bring. I am nothing if I am not a photographer with a bag of tricks. I remember the days when it was just me and Russell, who was my assistant for a long time, and we didn't have a lot. I didn't have the type of clients at that time who would pay for what my contemporary clients will pay for. There was no budget for rental equipment or extras. Now, whatever I put in the budget for expenses in terms of those things, the technical gadgets, it's covered.

However, in the early days, I wasn't even that experienced with the technical equipment, so we'd wing it. I think people liked that about us; we were funky. We had long, funky hair and never shaved, and we'd show up with a piece of a white cardboard box to use as a reflector and take pictures. We were clean though. We brushed our teeth.

This particular project with Aretha had really started six or seven years prior, when I shot her for the first time. I had been hired to do a shoot on a video she was making. They asked me to go to the set to photograph her, which is usually not a good situation because it's about the video or the movie, not about you and how you can get the picture you need.

Directors are, generally, not fond of still photographers and feel that we're sometimes amateur hacks. The crews often have an attitude, from the director on down; they tend to act like they're the greatest thing. My goal isn't to put down video directors – I have become one, at times – but there's maybe an insecurity that they're not film directors, thus, the arrogant attitude. Certainly, as a photographer you don't get a lot of respect from them. Therefore, this was not the best situation for me to walk into, but I did it because, God, it was *Aretha*...just to have that moment with her...

To meet Aretha Franklin, that, to me, was everything. I grew up with that music. There's great rap music; there's great pop music; there's great rock and roll; but I think the music that's going to make sense still to our great-great-grandchildren is Aretha and James Brown and other people. Our souls are different, *we* are different, because we heard that music, and they will live on because of that.

At that first shoot, I realized that there was a lot at work – a vibe, an undercurrent that everybody was running on. Aretha isn't your normal human being. She's a wonderful, amazingly talented woman, but you never know how she's going to behave or what she's going to do. She could walk at any minute. Now that I know her better, I find it endearing because there's a wonderful sort of crazy side to her that lends itself to great ideas. However, that day I was stuck and the only opportunity was going to be when she passed me on the way to catering. That was it; she would not be coming back. So I had a shot set up and asked her to just step into the frame; it took five minutes. That was it – my introduction to Aretha.

I guess when they showed the pictures to her, she liked them. She probably remembered it was quick and easy, that I hadn't hassled her because I got more calls to photograph her. Not long after, they asked me to come to Detroit to shoot her for an album cover. She's a funny woman, you know. She won't fly; she only takes buses. She cooks on the bus; she's got this kitchen set up with all her spices. So we had to go to Detroit because she didn't feel like traveling. We flew in a day or so early, and they said I needed to go to her house to look at clothes. It was July and sweltering and sticky. I think I've done twenty-five shoots in Detroit, and it's always in the summer and sweltering and sticky.

We showed up at her house, which is a large, upper-class, suburban kind of house, not a mansion, but a nice, big house. It's all white. She opened up the door in a bathing suit and gave me a hug. It was about 140 degrees in the house because she doesn't believe in air conditioning. It's not good for her voice or something like that. Everything was closed up, the windows, the drapes, everything. She was in a bathing suit, and there was like three feet of cleavage. I was sort of shocked, not at Aretha in her swimsuit, but at the whole experience, even now. I'm not easily star-struck – after all, this is what I do for a living – but there are some of these people, like Aretha, the legends, that just stop me dead. It's not nerves; it's this anticipation, this excitement, a recognition that I'm so glad to be here, that this is my life experience. I have records of hers from when she was like 14. Aretha is a personality who's got something that's coming from some place other than her publicist. There's a substance beyond what those of us mere mortals possess.

However, in that moment, I was thinking, "This is the stuffiest, hottest house I've ever been in!" And I was wearing all black, a sports jacket and jeans, and probably, at that time, cowboy boots. One look around the house and it was obvious that Aretha was ready for me to come. She had laid out her clothes – I'm talking 3,000 square feet, or whatever it was, on the first floor of the house, covered with clothes. There wasn't a place to stand. Literally, I tiptoed between outfits. I followed her into the kitchen, where she was cooking up something, and I had to tiptoe around hats and dresses and shoes. Aretha told me, "Sit down, Timothy. You want something to drink?" and I was thinking, I'm just this little white boy from New Jersey. What am I doing in Aretha Franklin's house, with her standing in her bathing suit, offering me a drink?

She showed me through the outfits, and she was digging through things, going through the closet and throwing boxes out behind her, saying things like, "You know I got the shoes to go with that," or "Timothy, would you come up and reach in the closet for me, dear?"...and this went on for two hours. I was soaking wet. I had ruined my jacket. It was the hottest place in the world.

We had found a historic mansion with formal gardens to rent and use for a location. The next day we were there setting up. She had been in hair and makeup for hours...the waiting, always the waiting. She came out in a Gucci black leather skirt and some hiking boots with fishnet stockings that she thought should be ripped. So she'd ripped them. This happens on shoots with Aretha. She does stuff like this and everyone kind of says, Okay. You don't argue with her. She's got her own idea of the way things should be and really, Who's going to tell her otherwise? I took pictures of Aretha in her ripped fishnet hose.

The thing about Aretha is that she's used to being in charge, though not in a bossy kind of way. She takes her time, and she calls it when she doesn't want to do something. She has her opinions, but she shows up, and she does the work to get the shoot done, and she takes suggestions. For the next shot, I had a location in mind. We moved outside into the formal gardens, really beautiful, lush, very structured gardens. I had the piano moved out onto the grass. She made an entrance – to put it mildly – in this yellow chiffon dress that was like a prom dress, with a big, poufy skirt – the whole deal. And there she was in this dress – this sleeveless, strapless, yellow prom dress that goes to the floor and on and on. I grabbed her by the hand, and I walked her over to where I saw the shot. We started shooting, and she started humming. I asked her if she would feel comfortable singing, explained that I'd love to hear her sing and asked if she would do that for me.

There's a moment in photography when a shoot can go from just working to magical. It's a matter of being prepared but then relaxing enough to let things happen, to not have too many preconceptions of what you want to get or how the day should go. If you leave yourself open, there will be something more special that comes out of it. Even with the knowledge and the bag of tricks and the experience, even with all of those techniques, there still needs to be room to let the magic happen. So there was Aretha, arms up in the air, singing for me. This was my moment, the split-second to get the picture I wanted of Aretha, the picture that would be one of those that defines who I am as a photographer. I was in heaven.

Four years passed since that shoot, and there I was with Aretha again. This time we were in another dramatic place: the Fox Theater in Detroit. She walked out in this pink fuckin' Vegas kind of showgirl thing with this big Dracula collar, almost like a head dress. It was the most bizarre outfit. And we were in this opulent theater, an old show palace kind of place, with big, rich, red-velvet seats and drapes.

We got some wonderful photographs of her, surrounded by velvet. Then she came out in this orange sequined number. When I see something like this, I'm like, Go, because she's so big, and I don't mean only in size – she's over the top – so go, go over the top, especially given our previous experience with the yellow dress. This took it to the next level. I had some concerns about how to top that picture. This was the topper. I posed her on the grand staircase in the orange number.

We needed one more picture. I got the theater people to put "Aretha Franklin-Sold Out" on the marquee and had her limo pull up right in front.

I perched up high on a ladder, and with the marquee slightly out of focus in the foreground, told her to step out of the limo, whenever she was ready. I didn't know what she was wearing, but that shiny white door swung open, and all I could see was one of those legs slide out. Slowly, she stepped out of the limo; she was in a trench coat and stockings – nothing else, that was it. She'd done it again.

Chapter 16
With A Little Help from My Friends

As my career started to take off, it was clear I needed help on set with my portrait photoshoots. Carrying heavy lighting equipment, stands, camera cases, and everything else to a shoot was becoming harder to manage on my own. I had friends who were helping me, but I couldn't lean on whoever was hanging around as I was building my career. It was time for me to find a qualified assistant and not just someone who could carry all the equipment needed on a shoot; I needed someone who could be my second set of eyes, to see where the light was hitting, to handle the little things as I managed the actual subject of the photo. This person needed to know what they were doing at the highest level of photography to handle the assignments that were coming in. The people I was shooting were becoming more important, and there was less room for error on each shoot.

In asking around, someone recommended a guy by the name of Russell Ward. Russell was older than most photo assistants, but younger than me, and also a constant cigarette and marijuana smoker. Although he was basically stoned all the time, he was very experienced and extremely competent. He was also a really cool dude. He had worked for every major fashion and portraiture photographer in New York City and Europe who was of any importance. He'd learned a lot about technique and all the tricks of the trade. In fact, he knew much more than I knew. As I didn't consider myself a technical guy, just someone who learned on the fly, I didn't really care to know or focus on that side of things, but I did know I had to up my game to the level of imagery I wanted to produce.

From the moment we started working together, we just fit. All of a sudden, Russell gave me security when we walked on set. He knew what to do, how to handle the equipment, how to really take accurate lighting readings, and he gave me the technical expertise that I personally didn't have. We instantly clicked because of our like-minded sensibilities; we were both rock 'n'roll types with our own expertise that worked together perfectly. Russell quickly became my right hand, my other eye. I could tell him what I wanted and direct him, and he knew how to bring what was in my head to life. He was also really into music in a way that I was too. We both listened to a lot of alternative genres, from African to South American music to world music in general, including Blues, R&B, and Soul. We would deep dive into music beyond the pop and rock and roll of the moment.

After a shoot, Russell would go home at night and record cassette tapes so that we had fresh music on set for the next day. He was the right blend of stoned and focused; he knew the good music and could turn it around on time before each shoot. We got to listen to the best music and, in turn, were also doing great photography. Everyone on our set felt that magic in the air, which allowed Russell and me to be in our own zones that made each shoot a success. I had this personality to engage people and get them to react to me in front of the camera, while Russell helped create the technical conditions that lead to "the shot" in a way I envisioned it in my mind. Our collaboration became a major turning point in my career.

For a long period of time, though, I sometimes felt inadequate next to Russell, as much as I relied on and loved him. I kept thinking, *God, this guy knows more than I know. Is it really about the light? What's he doing?*

Is this a great photo because of him or me? Of course, it was a great photo because of my own work, and of course Russell had the technical prowess to bring my vision into the world. The success of the shot wasn't solely on him, but it was a very big part, an equal part of what we accomplished as a team. Not only could I get the quality and level of professional lighting and technical expertise, but I also could be myself and do what I did because I knew he had his end together. Together as a team, we always had great music and a very professional, productive set that hummed like the songs we played.

There have been so many unique moments we've shared over our eight years working together, including managing and supporting our team as it grew. During that time, my career grew to the point where I was doing huge celebrity advertising jobs and ended up having three assistants. One was named TC, a friend of Russell's who became part of the team. Then there was Gus. My studio manager met Gus on the train in New York when he was 18 and going to art school. She introduced us, and he started to work at my studio. I had these three great guys with me, and we traveled everywhere together. Russell was in charge of that team, and he and I were aligned in such a way that he became even more than my right hand: he became my brother.

One weekend when we had a rare day off, I got a phone call from Russell's brother. He said Russell had a brain aneurysm the night before and died instantly. I was in shock.

After eight years together, it was a devastating loss for me, my staff, and for the team. I had lost my brother. In some ways, it was a loss for my identity, given Russell helped build my career from its early beginnings to a cover contract at *Rolling Stone* and helped us become capable of doing anything anywhere. Together, we prided ourselves in our ability to wing any situation. If it rained, we made it work. If it was too sunny, we found the bright side of the setup. No matter if it was inside on a set or outside on location, it didn't matter. We knew how to get the job done. That was the most important thing.

Immediately after Russell's funeral, I had to make a decision about how to move on. I went to TC, who then expressed to me that he didn't want to step into the first assistant role because he didn't want the responsibility of that position. In my grief over Russell's death, I wondered how I was also going to honor the legacy we had created, especially since bigger and bigger jobs continued to come in. With his passing, I lost some of my confidence and needed to get it back fast so I could move forward. My career was continuing to go through the roof, all while my team depended on me to keep things running. Continuing on in our work was something Russell would have wanted for us too.

While I was freaking out, I needed to know that I could walk on set the way I had done before and not have to think about any technical aspect except what I do best: Get my pictures. That's when I went to my third assistant, Gus. I liked the idea of this young guy taking the next step to becoming a top photo assistant; in photography you gradually build yourself up and then someday move into your own position and start taking your own pictures. However, Gus was a third assistant and would be skipping the second one and moving right to the top.

When we sat down to have this discussion, I knew he wasn't ready.

So did Gus.

However, it was the opportunity that made the most sense.

So, I turned to him and had to be honest with him.

"Gus, you know as well as I do that you are not up to the task and that you can't really fit Russell's shoes," I said. I know it sounded tough, but I didn't mean it disparagingly. I certainly didn't mean to insult him either because we both knew that Russell was a confident photo assistant and technician while Gus was still learning the ropes. However, Gus was smart and such a team player, and that counted for a lot. Gus was there for the team and would do anything and work as hard as anybody to make sure that things were done right.

"What's fair is that you get this opportunity," I continued, "but the truth of the matter is you're not up to it. So here's my plan. Go home, take photos, and do shoots every weekend. Shoot your mother, shoot the neighbors. I don't care what it is, but do it. Take Polaroids and show me the film. Show me you have a handle on the technological aspect of what we need to do so we can go onto a set and be in charge and accomplish what we need to do for each shoot."

Gus, with his usual grit and commitment to the team, agreed to do just that. Although I could tell he was insecure about the opportunity – and, honestly, so was I – I had to come to terms with learning how to move on without Russell. It was not a comfortable situation.

Gus went home and then started coming into the studio that first week with pictures he was taking at night and over the weekend. He was doing his homework, and at some point, it broke my heart that I'd given him this assignment at all. He was clearly a dedicated guy, and it didn't seem fair to have him continue proving himself.

"You know what," I finally said, after Gus had been doing this for two weeks, "forget it. You're in. Let's just do it, man. Let's just jump in the water and learn how to swim. Once we get in there, I know we can do this."

It was like the greatest trust fall: we jumped and never looked back. Not only did he rise to the occasion, becoming the best in the business as a first assistant, he became my best friend and someone I could count on and share my life with. He became a soulmate. I've spent more hours in airplanes, shared more meals, and experienced more unique opportunities with Gus than anyone else in my life – I mean, more than my parents, my siblings, and even my wife.

Gus and I have now been together for over 30 years. Although he's now a great photographer in his own right, we still work together. It's still as seamless as it ever was. Over the years, Gus has still been the same dedicated man we met on the subway; he's never had an ego and can be on set and can be quietly in charge. We used to have this ethos between us where we said, "Being prepared on a photoshoot was like thinking ahead in baseball. If I'm playing second base and there's men on base, and if the ball comes to me, what do I do? I don't know where it's going, but if it comes to me, who do I throw it to first? Do I throw it to the shortstop at second? Do I throw it to the pitcher? Do I throw it to home plate? What do I do depending on the circumstances that are in front of me?"

That's the way Gus was on set. He had a 180 degree...maybe more... 270-degree peripheral vision. He always knew what was going on. The thing that resonates most in my memory is being on set over the years, standing on a ladder or an apple box, up high with my tripod directing the set, looking through my camera trained on my subject and calling out, "Gus, do we have it?" "Gus, are you there?" meaning...Did he have that light just right... Did the subject look good...Were we ready to shoot...Was he in the right spot at the right time?

And he always was.

Chapter 17

In the Studio With...

In my NYC photography studio, I was creating something that felt very true to me: a chosen family who loved each other as much as they bickered and laughed; friends who had been in the photography studios of legends like Irving Penn, Patrick Demarchelier, and Richard Avedon and knew that I was focused on creating an entirely different dynamic. Demarchelier was the king, and everybody stayed quiet. You worked around him, worshipped him, and adored him. It was the same with Irving Penn and with Avedon. However, in my studio, when you were there, you were family. You could walk in and a Hollywood star would just be leaving, and they'd be hugging and kissing my staff goodbye because they knew my team and felt so at home.

The most important part was that everyone in the studio was kind and fun. In some way we were a group of dysfunctional misfits. There was TC, a tall, skinny guy, who looked like a cowboy and wore rings on every finger and actually lived in the studio for a couple of years; he smoked cigarettes and weed constantly but was always on top of it and assumed the role of the studio caretaker. Then there was Mark, this guy from London, who had a cheeky sense of humor and had a habit of exposing himself for fun and trying to always shock us. *What was that about?!* That wouldn't fly nowadays, of course, but it was the 90s and early 2000s and anything went. There was Cliff, my retoucher/printer, whom I relied on for everything digital, clearly the brains of the outfit; however, he often fell asleep at his computer while working, which kept me constantly vigilant and on top of him. There was Sara, my studio manager, who was the sweetest young woman, who looked about 12 but was in charge of the studio and this mangy bunch and handled the business thoroughly. Gus, my devoted assistant, who became like a brother to me and had no ego, was always so focused on getting the job done right; I know I couldn't have done it without him. He and I have worked together for over 30 years now, and we have traveled more miles and have had more unique experiences together than anyone in my life. I owe him so much for the great work and the times we've shared. Just to mix this gang up was my bookkeeper of many years, Elizabeth, a Black woman who preached her Christian values – more on that later. At the time, Elicia was still my wife and my acting creative director and always on the phone and spinning the plates with the staff. I was flanked by all my assistants, always cordial and the buffer that kept me in my zone of creativity.

The business of the studio at that time was energetically intense. We'd come in for the next shoot, and whether it was a big-name actor or a young rock star, my crew would all be joking, laughing and partying. If we had a night shoot, I would still shoot all day and then continue all night. I paid for it all, and it was just one big party, where we'd order food, beer, laugh, and just roll into one shoot after another. I ran the studio as a very happy set. How could I not? We were a part of something exciting, and we could all feel it. People came to my studio for a big job, expecting the shoot to be about me and them, but it was really about the family of the photography studio. I created a team that was fun, quirky, and capable. I had the ability to be focused and personable, yet I always paid attention to my surroundings and what was in front of me. Basically, I staged my studio the way I grew up: One big crazy family.

On all my shoots, whether in my studio or on location, everybody had a voice. Everybody could speak up. Everybody could be a part of it. Everybody loved each other. The celebrity of the shoot would walk in, and they'd see us laughing. They were immediately at ease and part of the family instead of the star of the show. They'd watch me and the stylist walk through the clothes, seeing this open dialogue between us. It would turn the celebrity's brain on in a special way, giving them license to play with us. In playing, you get the most human, playful, available moment in time – and pictures that endure.

Once you get experienced enough as a photographer, you know how to create the mood and feeling you want to have on the set – with the light, the music, the catering, props and with the right team of assistants – but the key is catching moments. The best photos you've seen are about catching moments. Imagine Shirley MacLaine looking in the mirror as I walk into the dressing room before the shoot and I catch that moment; even if we set it up, it made her feel like we were doing something unique, spontaneous and fast. My spontaneity made my subjects feel involved, and we would end up laughing, crying, bonding, and always getting something special.

Living between the shots is exactly what I learned, after so many years, and tried to impart to my studio family. My subject would pose; I'd stop, laugh, react, have a genuine human moment before the next shot. I'd make a joke; they'd pose and smile, and then maybe say something serious; and I'd get a straight look and shoot again. It's a healthy manipulation that a photographer uses. However, he needs to also be present on the set to see the vulnerability in the subject and then to also see how to stick the knife in, twist it, and dig it out...and then give everybody a lollipop at the end. It was a treat for everyone.

I admitted something to myself a long time ago. It's the reason I often say I'm more a psychologist than a photographer. I look at a celebrity through my lens, and I work with them, charming, schmoozing, flirting and laughing. It's comic timing and directing people's reactions, and it's all from reading someone's eyes. I can see when I'm losing them, when they're bored, when they're distracted, when they're with me, when they're too intense – whatever their mood is, I can tell by looking in their eyes. The eyes are my total focus. They are what make the connection between the two of us. They are the signal for whether I act or react. They are the key to finding what works at that moment.

All my shoots throughout the years live in my mind as a carousel of moments. I remember fragments of each photoshoot: the cigar clenched between Arnold Schwarzenegger's teeth while the light highlighted his chiseled face and gently lit up his eyes; the back of Whoopi's long dreads as she twirled on the roof; the sweet quality of Audrey Hepburn, one of the biggest actors ever, who trustingly allowed this young kid to direct her through a photo session. All of these pieces twinkle like blinking Christmas lights in the lens of my memory, moments both technical and profound. That combination of art, technicality, and tenacity is what allowed me to get the shots that will live on forever. What follows is a short version of a "shot list" of people who have wafted through my doors and left an indelible impression on my heart – and perhaps yours, too – and the themes that came up constantly in the studio during shoots and what I learned from them.

Whitney Houston and Her Mother Cissy

Nothing can truly contain my dear friend and longtime collaborator of more than 30 years, celebrity stylist Wayne Scot Lukas. He has a unique and wild personality. If you talk to either of us, you'll get two different answers about how we met. I joked it was on the subway, but he actually has the right answer. Wayne was a young fashion stylist, new to New

York City, and a mutual friend said she'd try to get a meeting between the two of us. Wayne didn't know anything about me, apparently, and came up to the studio for the meeting. He says I was wearing "tiny, red, satin coochie shorts with white trim, short as could be, all the way up your butt, and thick white socks and clogs and a tank top. Sort of 1990's Richard Simmons." *Yikes! Really?* I was a runner and would leave the studio to get in my miles in between shoots, and I guess he must have walked in just after. *What a memory.*

While Wayne could clearly size up anyone's outfit in record time, I thought he was handsome, crazy, fun, open, and very welcoming, the perfect vibe for my studio. Our chemistry was instant.

However, that wasn't actually the first time we met. We actually met on the set for a *Rolling Stone* shoot featuring Whitney Houston and her mother, Cissy Houston. At the time, Wayne was an assistant to Patti Wilson, an iconic fashion stylist who was working consistently with Whitney on many other shoots and a series of music videos. This was my first time shooting Whitney, who of course acted like the star of the moment, and Cissy, the proud mother, was there to do whatever Whitney wanted.

So we put them both in leather motorcycle jackets, and as we were getting ready to shoot, Wayne went to my office, found some white nail polish and came back to the set and painted the word "Mommy" on Cissy's lapel and "Whitney" on hers. I mean right on her new borrowed leather jacket like it was embroidery. It made the picture so perfect and created a fun energy with everybody around the shoot.

For the record, photographers and stylists are the peanut butter and jelly of creative photography relationships; Wayne was – and still is – for me. We learned to depend on each other. It's a deeper connection. We've had each other's backs for years. Even if a client sucks or there's not a big budget, we know we're going to have a ball on set and many stories to share for years to come.

Being Present with Mary Tyler Moore

Once during an intimate shoot with Mary Tyler Moore, we started talking about being in relationships, and I said to her, "Oh, what you're saying is so moving." She replied, "I remember when I broke up with my first husband," and all of a sudden, the tears started to flow down her face, and I grabbed that shot. The connection we were sharing would not have happened if, as the photographer, I was just saying, "Turn right...Turn left...Fix that hair." You get it from those special moments because you're present. If you're smart enough, when the world unfolds around you as a photographer, you catch glimpses of those amazing moments that nobody else sees because my team and I stay present and aware of everything happening around us. I was never not working on a set even though it seemed like I was playing. Everyone else would be thinking I was only having fun, but I was catching every little detail.

If it was somebody's broken fingernail, if it was the ring they were wearing, if it was the guitar pick they used when they wrote their last song... I saw everything and made it a part of the image of them. I may not have even been present all the time in my personal life, but I was present all the time in my professional one. That may be where the disconnect was with Elicia and why life got weirdly tough because being present at work often meant you couldn't be present at home. It could all be so exhausting, and the constant focus on my career kept life quickly moving forward.

Robin Williams and Nathan Lane

I shot this duo in Manhattan in 1995 for their movie *The Birdcage*. Our goal was to create the movie poster, but we got so much more that day. The prop stylist on the shoot brought lipsticks, robes, pillows, bird cages of all sizes – some big enough to stand in. There was a huge pile of props. The entire shoot was instantaneous as Robin kept grabbing props, doing something for the camera, tossing it back, grabbing another. I just kept shooting for two hours straight. He was on fire, and I wasn't about to stop the creativity from flowing. Nathan just giggled along and let Robin's genius rule the shoot. The next day, my face hurt from laughing and smiling so much. After Robin and Nathan had a pillow fight that filled the studio with feathers, Robin, always so aware of comedic nuance, took a single feather, gently placed it in his mouth, and looked straight at the camera with an expression like the cat who got the canary. Despite the enormous amount of great material from that day, that one image said it all.

Glenn Close

I'll admit, working with actresses can be tricky. Some are intimidated by the still camera, singularly focused on them. Instead, they're used to the constantly moving motion picture camera where they don't have to focus on or address it directly. However, those with theater backgrounds can be more comfortable with being in front of a still camera and generally avoid its stare. Glenn was one of those people. We got to know each other and did many shoots together. We did a session at her house in Bedford, New York, where the scene was perfectly picturesque: Glenn on her swing, hanging from a tree, dressed in a beautiful gold lamé gown; sharing a special moment with her horse in the stable, strolling down a grassy hill in her backyard as her cat followed her. There we were, doing this sweet, wholesome shoot with her animals in her home. It was this really intimate day. Then, when we walked back into her house, I was confronted by one of her most famous props: A giant knife from her role in *Fatal Attraction* in a frame right there against the kitchen backsplash – quite the juxtaposition.

Robert Mitchum

It was 1988. I was doing photographs for different magazines and started to shoot album covers and other important assignments; I felt like things were starting to happen for me and that I was building on a career. I was going all around to appointments and trying to get people to know who I was and that I was an active photographer, but I just didn't feel that I was being as creative as I wanted to be. I felt a little intimidated by my peers who I thought all had some sort of distinct vision, or at least had a picture that was theirs, so to speak, one that represented their unique, quintessential point of view. In some ways, I think that's part of the insecurity of being an artist: There is security and freedom in what you do, but you're always second guessing yourself and wondering if you're doing your best work. I plowed forward, though, and kept taking pictures and getting assignments and building my career.

I got a call from *US Magazine* to go and shoot Robert Mitchum. Well, my background of sitting at home late at night as a young teenager, smoking cigarettes and watching *The Late Show*, immersed in old black-and-white movies of the thirties and forties, especially the genre of *film noir*, made me ready to meet my favorite actor. There was this love affair I had with Robert Mitchum; I just thought he was the coolest. Knowing how irreverent he was and that he was arrested for marijuana possession in 1949 and all of that stuff just really made me dig his character a lot.

In any case, I was sent up to Santa Barbara to do the shoot with him, which is where he lived. I was told to meet him at a local hotel and that we could shoot on the property. So I got in the car with my assistant, and we drove up to Santa Barbara with our equipment and showed up at this hotel. I had no idea where he was, and I was looking around trying to find him. It was the middle of the afternoon, and I walked into the restaurant to find him sitting at the bar with two empty martini glasses in front of him and another one in his hand.

I introduced myself and, of course, he looked up at me, not knowing who I was at first. I'm guessing the man was in his seventies at that time, and I was probably thirty or so and looking all scruffy and ratty and youthful, though genuinely enthused to meet one of my heroes and to get to work with him. I was not only in love with his movies, but one in particular tied us together: *Thunder Road*, which was also a song and an important piece for me by my other hero, Bruce Springsteen. In fact, I even bought the original movie poster and had it framed in my studio. So this was a significant moment getting the opportunity to shoot him.

He seemed nice enough, a little grumpy, a little gruff, but we exchanged pleasantries and introductions, and I said I was going to go outside and set something up, look for the shot, and come back and get him when I was ready. Apparently, there was a publicist coming, and then later I found out his son came up for the shoot as well. However, at that moment, I ran out to go set something up, and after I formed the lighting and composition for my shot, I went to retrieve my subject. We did some pictures, but for some reason nothing from the first set up really enthused me. I'm never really intimidated by the people I photograph, but there was definitely a nervousness, working with one of my heroes.

I began to set up a second shot in the parking lot, and he and his publicist were there, talking with his son and the writer from the magazine. They were standing and talking, and I was behind them setting up with my assistant. My assistant whispered, "Hey, look!" I looked around and saw his publicist was in front of him, and he was behind her. While they were talking to the writer who was in front of her, we saw that Robert Mitchum was grabbing her butt and pinching her, and she was swatting his hand away with her hand. This was all unbeknownst to the writer or anyone else, but because we were behind them, we could see what was really going on.

Anyway, that's just a little anecdote about the kind of man he was.

As we started to shoot and I saw the first Polaroid, something clicked for me, and I instantly recognized a different look, a different something, that just went right through me and gave me the willies because I had hit on something and I knew it. The picture was just a tight headshot of him, but the nature of my lighting, the composition, and the direction of our interaction looked different. What I captured showed me a way to photograph someone that was inspiring. It hit me right away. I was not just taking a picture but, in fact, *making* a picture that was different. It was an epiphany for me that made me realize that, from that point forward,

I needed to focus on my work in a different way. And it wasn't just throwing up a light and making sure I got that person on film. Instead, it was somehow filming that person and drawing something out of them that was a technical and visionary interaction; it was a clear distinction from how I approached picture taking previously and a major moment for my career. It became a turning point; from that point forward, I went into every shoot looking for that new opportunity to transform and to take what was straightforward and in front of me and make it a part of my new vision.

Paul McCartney

When The Beatles hit in 1964, it was a big deal. I grew up with two older sisters who were young teens through the British invasion, playing their music through the house constantly. My boyhood friend Robby and I experienced it through our older siblings, and we pretended we were The Beatles, listening to their music in my parents' basement, using tennis rackets as guitars. I was always John, and he was Paul. Twenty-eight years later, *Rolling Stone* called me to shoot Paul for the magazine while on his US tour. *Do you think this was a big deal for me?!*

My concept was "Paul McCartney on the road." My assistants and I flew to Chicago to meet up with his entourage. He was performing for four nights at a local arena, and I had total access before, during, and after the show to get the images I needed for the magazine cover and inside pages. We were staying at the same hotel, and every day we were packed and ready to follow his team to the venue, hoping to pull the vehicles to the side of the road and grab the cover shot I had in mind of Paul "on the road." I never knew when he was coming or going. Waiting to find out if that was possible and when he would come down to leave for sound check was very difficult. With that much security, it was like being with a president...it was not easy access. We'd sit outside the hotel with our equipment in a minivan for hours. It was freezing; I mean, it was winter in Chicago. Whenever he walked out, we had to be ready. We couldn't eat; we couldn't pee; we had one job: Wait for Paul. Every day for four days, we waited, and every day his security would come out to our van and say, "Not today." We'd then go to the venue, shoot sound check, backstage, portraits of Paul and his wife Linda, which was really great stuff, but I still didn't get my cover. Every day, I thought, "Today I'm going to get him on the side of the road," and I was so hyped up on adrenaline with the whole experience, especially to get my *Rolling Stone* cover of Paul.

Night four ended, and I still didn't have the shot.

He was leaving the next day, and his team told me that we'd get the opportunity I wanted on the way to the airport and to follow his motorcade. So we tailed his limo with our van and waited for his people to stop and tell me when. At a red light, his security hopped out of the car ahead and said that they just didn't have the time. We weren't going to get it. I was so frustrated. I had two days to get to Boston and be ready for the next cover with Billy Joel. My editor told me to forget it and move on to Boston; I probably had other potential cover shots from the week. But this was everything to me. My childhood fanaticism with The Beatles, shooting Paul for the *Rolling Stone*. I wanted my cover!

The security guy said that if I wanted to jump on the plane with Paul, he would guarantee me the shot the next day in Toronto – no assistants though, no major equipment, just me jumping on the plane – and I had to be ready when we got to the airport to just go. I had about 3 minutes tops to get it together. I stuffed film, filters, my camera – anything that I could into my pockets – as we pulled through the gate and up to the private plane. I told my assistants to go on to Boston on their own and that I would meet them there in a couple of days. I had to get my shot.

I ran up the steps to the plane. The door closed, and I was there with Paul and Linda...just us...and I was freaking out inside. I shot pictures of them on the plane and tried to be as unobtrusive as possible. When we landed sometime late that night, we all went to the hotel and up to our rooms. I was so hyped up by my experience and had trouble resisting the urge to call everyone from high school to tell them what I was doing.

The next morning I got the call. I came down to the lobby and jumped in one of the cars with security. We were headed somewhere – I didn't know – and we barreled up a ramp toward the highway. I had no idea what it looked like on the other side, but security asked me where, and I just said "Now...go up this ramp...and pull over right here!" Paul jumped out, and I directed him to stand with his guitar on the side of the road, hitchhiking in some of the shots. Morning commuters were driving by, and at least some had to recognize the famous Beatle. I shot a few rolls of film – so fast – but I knew that I had it. I finally got my cover shot.

Julian Lennon

Julian Lennon and I have been close friends for over 38 years. We met early in our careers – he had just finished his successful and groundbreaking album, *Valotte*, and I was hired to shoot the publicity photos for his music video. We hit it off right away, and I went on to shoot his next two album covers and photograph him repeatedly over the years. My connection to The Beatles runs deep, and, as I've already mentioned, John was my favorite. Building a friendship with Julian felt incredibly natural, despite all the history of growing up with his father's music. I saw the weight that he carried living in the shadow of a father who was more famous than famous, and yet Julian paved his own path. He lost his dad in so many ways: First to fame, then to separation and divorce, and ultimately to a bullet. Through a lot of it, we've been friends and support systems for one another. I've helped to support him in a photography career, and he has helped me with my own creativity. I saw that photography was something that could be his own, where he wouldn't be compared to his dad. That shared passion became a big part of our bond.

Fate has a way of weaving these connections in my life. Early on, after John's death, *Rolling Stone* magazine hired me to photograph Yoko Ono and her young son, Sean. Years later, I was with Julian in New York and asked him if he would help me bring him and Sean together for a rare photo. Although both were reluctant, they agreed. They didn't see each other that often, but they agreed, for each other, and for me. This is something that I do often. I bring people together for a portrait to capture a moment for posterity that wouldn't happen otherwise...fathers and sons, estranged partners, brothers, sisters...taking a picture that I know has historical significance and needs to be taken. We had a hotel room at the Ritz Carlton in New York, and I asked them both to dress formally in evening wear. I used my large, tedious 8x10 camera for the slow and studied nature of the process and had them in a sort of after-party, casual mood, standing in a doorway and leaning on each other. The pose seemed to signify their position in life and how much they needed each other.

Some day, 20 years from now, maybe 30, if they don't already, I hope they will realize how important that image is: The Lennon brothers, *together*, two musicians, each carving their own legacy, when for some the legend of their last name would say enough.

Chapter 18
Pin-ups

The Vargas pin-ups homage started somewhere around 1994 when *Esquire* came to me – I was under contract to them as a photographer – and asked if I knew who Vargas was. Of course I did. They said that he had started out doing these illustrations in *Esquire* in the 1940s, and they wanted to bring back the Vargas pin-ups for the 1990s. However, they wanted to recreate his work through photographs instead of illustrations. *Would I be interested in doing it?*

Absolutely.

I started researching to find out what had been so special about Vargas's work and how I could in some way reproduce that special feeling. Illustration has creative license. Whatever is in the artist's mind can be created. With the Vargas illustrations, all of the clothes are transparent, so you see all the nuances of a woman's body – the muscle tone, shapes and textures of skin – through the transparent clothes in a way that you would never see in a photograph. I mean, yes, you could put lingerie on and wet it down and you would get some of the muscle tone and the bone structure, but it still wouldn't be what those illustrations were.

This was right around the time of the famous Demi Moore *Vanity Fair* cover where she was entirely painted, and I was kind of intrigued by the idea of body paint, but not the way that cover was done. That looked to me like somebody whose body had been painted – nothing more, nothing less. I wanted something that was more three-dimensional, more about fantasy, but the idea of the paint seemed connected, somehow, to what was achieved with illustrations. So, I thought, "Well, what if we take pieces of clothing and actually use some of the fabric, glue it to the body, along with the body paint?" We did a test and realized it could work but discovered that the way to really fine-tune it, to make these amazing fantasy girls like the Vargas pin-ups, was with digital retouching. That way, no one else could reproduce what we came up with. It would be entirely our own.

Like the Vargas illustrations, they were illusions; they were fantasy. I would never retouch someone in my celebrity portraiture like we can with this technology. It would be going too far. It was okay for us to go beyond with the *Esquire* centerfolds because they were about creating an illusion – perfect fantasy women. We could do anything, go crazy, as long as it was within the realm of what was aesthetically pleasing to me and the potential *Esquire* readers. I wanted to maintain elements of the photographic look but take it over the top.

Before body positivity was a thing, we'd edit these photos within an inch of their lives. I'd whiten their eyes or enhance their eye color or add hair or straighten their teeth or thin their waistline or add a curve to their thighs, calves, do a better pedicure or change their toes or change the nail polish color. I'd take arms out, move or adjust a boob if it didn't fit at the right angle. It made me look more closely, to come in close on every single aspect of the body, from the fingernails to the shoulder, from the top of head to top of the toe, to go through every aspect of the body and tweak. "I don't like that birthmark there, but maybe it would look cool over there...

There's a shadow here that I don't want, but I want more shadow in her cleavage...Get rid of those little creases at the ankle..." No, it's not real – none of it is real – but your mind's eye won't really notice that. What it will notice is how perfect she is. It made me think how neurotic we'd be if all of us had one of these things in our bathroom mirrors, so that the first thing we'd do every morning is tweak our image.

When *Esquire* hired me for this homage to Vargas, it was meant to be a one-time thing. Instead, it became a big deal, and it went on for 18 issues. It started with this wonderful model, Amber Smith, who was completely open to the idea. At that point, we were having to work to get models to do this with us because it was eight hours of basically being naked and having your body painted. It wasn't the best job for a model; however, that was only at the beginning. When everyone saw the results, it became hugely popular. We started getting press everywhere, from *Page Six* to *TMZ* and all the networks.

Supermodels wanted to do it. Cindy Crawford, Stephanie Seymour, Naomi Campbell, Elle Macpherson all wanted to be the next Vargas girl, to be the *Esquire* centerfold. It was the perfect image for *Esquire*. It wasn't vulgar; it was sexy.

We created outfits that were inspired by and patterned after a Vargas image, but we made them our own, more modern. My stylist and creative partner, Wayne Scot Lukas, who borrowed clothing and jewelry from Cartier or whomever, got this amazing artist to airbrush the paint on the models. On one model we painted capri pants on her body, including painting on the little drop shadow at the seam so it looked multi-dimensional. She had on only half a hat, a brim that was actually a straw floor mat that, at the right angle, looked like a hat. We just glued the ribbon onto the back of her hair and draped it over. The rest of the figure was all either body paint or things we added digitally. I considered this one a success because it really made the viewer do a double take. It had the surreal quality I was looking for.

In another, we created stockings, a garter, and underwear all with the computer. In one a little panty was painted right onto her body, sprayed through lace. We then glued a see-through fabric as a skirt over it. One model was wearing nothing but jewels. We took thousands of little rhinestones and glued them onto her and then blended in real pieces of jewelry that created a fantastic, glimmering illusion. Sometimes we would end up using a different shot of her face, literally transferring the face from one photo onto her body from another, because I liked her expression in one and her pose in another.

Now, of course, you get why this project was really about control and why it was a turn-on to me. It was the one thing that I was totally in control of, beyond even my photography. The editor didn't get to pick the image – I might shoot 100 frames but only give the magazine one – because my team and I just put 40 hours into the fucking thing...and that's to finish *one* of them, to create *one* fantasy girl. To do more, I would have had to work on another frame, and each one would be different. It's so subjective, so time consuming, so work intensive. However, each image was one of a kind – in essence, it's back to what Vargas was doing – the result of a personal vision. It was a way to create something that was unique...and entirely mine.

The transition from the original frame to the revised final image can blow your mind. We literally work almost pixel by pixel to make these changes. I can change one curl in her hair, move one freckle. It could take eight hours to get her ready and 15 minutes to shoot her, but those 15 minutes are all we need to get the idea of the image. Then, it's all the post-shoot work.

In a weird way, this whole process made me look at people differently. We would sit for hours and look at the screen, scrutinizing someone's skin, someone's eyes, someone's toes and think, "God those toes are funky... That skin should be smoothed...Let's lift that eyebrow." We focused so intensely that it was hard to come away from it and then look at a person without doing the same thing. I look at someone through my lens now, and

I think, I would do this or move that hair. It's not reality by any means, but it's a way of scrutinizing and looking more closely than I ever did before.

With portraiture, it's about the moment. It's about being reactionary, something that happens when the light hits right and the subject walked out in that outfit and the dog ran over to them and they laughed and I clicked. It's all about waiting for something to happen and trying to capture something that's real within the contrived setting of photography. The pin-ups were not about personality or the illusion of reality; it was just all about fantasy.

Clearly, I was not the only one playing around with this hyper-manipulation. Way back whenever, there was this idea that a picture never lied. Now, it's like, of course the picture lies! Really, though, it always did; it's just that now we're aware of it. Just the act of pushing the shutter at a decisive moment is subjective editing; what went on the second before and the second after are different from that second you chose to click.

In a sense, that is editing and that is control, the creation of an illusion, a lie, a manipulation of photographic truth, if you will, of truth in general. Now, it's simply happening more so. I think the average person is savvy about these things because we're faced with fantastic imagery every day that can't possibly be real, yet we buy into it because we're so entrenched and drenched with a false sense of reality and the perfect filtered image.

Is it a negative thing to have all of this artifice in our lives, in photography? It's different, certainly, than what it was, but if you're talking about celebrities, celebrities can be perfect. We want our heroes that way. It is about perfection. We accept it as such. We eat it up. I don't think we want our celebrities to be ugly or imperfect. We want them pure. That's our fantasy; that's our illusion. In a society that sees disease, war, starvation, drugs, we want our celebrities to be perfect. There's a lot of pressure here to keep playing the game, and so we do. It's more fun that way... certainly for me.

Admitting how I work with celebrities and get them to react to me is something I'm very conscious of. With models I don't have to be so manipulative. The model/photographer relationship is different. We're both trying to use our experience and craft to work together and mold something that we both know is not real. We're both wearing our masks to create an illusion. In some way, we're both doing a dance that is less personal than with celebrities. The model is allowing me to mold them to a vision and is not trying to hold onto who they really are. It's all an illusion, and it's about sculpture and clay. Both subjects are exciting, and when there is a collaboration from a celebrity to allow us both to manipulate the moment, like with a model, sometimes that becomes magic.

This might lead you to wonder how I got involved in this pin-up project, a concept that, on the face of it, was all about the models. Looking back now at the 18 months of *Esquire* centerfolds, I can understand how someone would take that perspective, but that would be missing the larger point. No, while the pin-ups seemed to be about famous models and T&A, what they were really about for me was creativity...and control. It was also a return to when I was snapping photos of aspiring models in the early days, using what I learned there on a larger stage.

Chapter 19

God Bless You

Sometime around 1990, I managed to connect with new representation in New York City through an agency by the name of Stockland/Martel. Stockland/Martel represented some photographers that I saw as having a more elevated roster than the agent I was working with in Los Angeles at the time. Although the agent in Los Angeles had really connected me in Hollywood, I wanted to branch out even more in Hollywood as well as in New York's larger editorial and commercial advertising campaigns. Although change and breakups are difficult for me, I decided to make the transition.

I quickly developed a really strong relationship with the agency and started to make a lot more money for myself and for Stockland/Martel as I perpetuated my Hollywood career as well as my New York advertising gigs. As we started to work together and the jobs got bigger and bigger, more money was flowing through my account, and my bookkeeper and accountant, whom I had started with earlier on in my career, were not quite up to the task and the level of photography and business that I was now getting into. Stockland/Martel had a bookkeeper working for them by the name of Elizabeth, a Christian Black woman who was personable and very sweet. We developed a strong relationship as we exchanged financials back and forth between estimates for jobs and then final budgets, invoices, and then finally collecting on those invoices.

As I developed this relationship with Elizabeth, it seemed that she was so much more in tune with the ins and outs of working the budgets for the commercial jobs that we were acquiring, and it just seemed natural that, given she wasn't working full time for Stockton/Martel, she could work part-time for me. As that relationship grew over the years, there was a lot more money flowing through my photography business, along with the bookkeeping related to the real estate I was buying and the associated construction and renovations. Therefore, Elizabeth became more and more a part of my life and my studio, working more hours for me to the point where she was now a full-time part of my studio staff.

My studio had a number of employees as well as freelance people. At the time, Elicia and I had a large apartment on W. 37th St. in Manhattan that I had renovated, and I also had my new studio building on 54th Street. I had a home in the Hamptons and a larger warehouse there for my growing collection of cars. All of this required the in and out of monies and paying of bills, taxes, and utilities. There were so many little details for all of these properties and then, of course, my insane acquisition of Amboy in the middle of the desert in California. Between all of the plane flights and all of the bills and all of the employees, and all the freelancers and all the expenses and the mortgages and the different facets of business...I needed more attention to my accounting, and Elizabeth fit that bill. She continued to work part-time with Stockland/Martel but quickly became a part of my studio family.

As my business grew and my life changed so much over the years, Elizabeth was there for all of the growth and all of the changes, both professionally and personally, that were going on in my life. In 2008 there was a big economic crisis in this country, and my advertising business dried up overnight.

I then very quickly lost all of my savings in the stock market. I had a million dollars in investments, and in rapid succession, that money was gone. Over the course of weeks, I was left holding the bag on large pieces of property and mortgages as well as salaries and all of the things that made up my financial portfolio and my financial world in general.

It quickly became a difficult financial nightmare to juggle. What had quickly gone from a very lucrative business had become me now struggling for income. My drive to generate revenue was my main concern, yet it seemed to have come to a standstill. In the middle of it all, my marriage collapsed. On top of that, I had to lay off long-term employees and handle the pressures of my financial responsibilities.

The one person who needed to continue to be there with me to keep all the balls in the air was Elizabeth. I needed someone to try and keep track of things that I was trying to juggle and keep my life from collapsing every day.

In the good times, I used to buy lunch for everyone at the studio, and there were a couple of tables at one end of the studio floor where we all sat and had lunch. Although it may have been frivolous, it just seemed like something that I wanted to do for my team. Those meals seemed to keep everybody working together and allowed me to kind of keep an eye on them, if you will. We were all there, relaxed and having fun, and it was part of the family atmosphere. It was also a way for me to keep the machine working and not have everyone going in different directions and becoming distracted.

However, after things started to collapse and employees had to leave the business, plus Elicia and I had separated – it eventually became just Elizabeth and me. We would sit and have lunch in the afternoon, and I was usually worried and stressed. I had lost long-term employees. I had lost the lucrative nature of my business and the freedom that came with that. I was struggling with mortgages. I had a $5 million mortgage on my studio building, and with the economic crisis, that bank went out of business.

The bank president, who was my friend and was helping me from defaulting on my mortgage with delayed payments during those difficult times, ended up going to prison for bank fraud. There was a lot of difficulty in the financial world at that time, and I was at the center of it because of the amount of debt and the amount of money that was going in and out of my life when the bank went under.

The bank sat in limbo for a while, and the FDIC eventually took it over. Consequently, my large monthly payment on a $5 million mortgage was on hold. This being a bad time, when I really didn't have the money, I was sort of blessed with not having to pay that mortgage.

However, after a number of months, that grace period came to an end as the FDIC eventually sold the bank's holdings to a hedge fund. When the hedge fund took over, they came to me and said, not only did I owe the mortgage, but they didn't want to hold the mortgage any longer and wanted all of their money back.

Not only did I not have the $5 million to pay them back, but I couldn't get another mortgage at that time. It was a difficult moment for that kind of transaction, certainly for somebody who was underwater like I was. It became a battle between the new owners of the bank and me, which ended up becoming a very contentious lawsuit, which again took me to a place with a lot of additional legal bills.

I had a lawyer who was negotiating with the new bank management, but at one point I had to go to a bankruptcy lawyer because I needed to threaten the bank to signal they were going to lose completely because I was going to go bankrupt. Truthfully, though, I did not want to go bankrupt because of so many other aspects of my financial life that I didn't want to suffer and was still trying to keep afloat. Nonetheless, I still needed to have that threat with the bank. Thus, I had my general counsel, my litigators who were threatening and working with the bank lawsuit, and then bankruptcy counsel that were working together with the litigators to try and bring down this lawsuit and this threat from the bank to foreclose. At the same time, not having the business revenue, losing my assistants and the people who helped me keep it all afloat – compounded by my marriage collapsing – became quite a lot to handle.

We can certainly say that this was a difficult time for me, and it was a constant struggle. The building was worth probably $10 million before the economic collapse. I had 5 million in it, which was the mortgage amount. I bought it for three, and I put a million and a half into it. However, the building was worth a lot more than that. Given the economic collapse and the collapse of real estate values in New York City, even though I tried to sell the building and get out from under my debt, I was getting offers from bottom feeders of $3 and $4 million for a building that I knew was worth much more.

At one point, the building, which I meticulously renovated, was written up in *Architectural Digest* magazine. I was very proud of this beautiful home, for both my archive and my image in general. My face as a well-known, successful celebrity photographer needed to be maintained in order to continue to do the work that I do. No one wants to hire somebody when they're down and out. I managed a facade to keep myself floating, but at the same time, my debt got deeper and deeper as the lawyers got deeper and the bills got higher. My fragile emotional state grew, as I struggled to maintain not only my image but my lifestyle and my encumbrances while still trying to take care of everything in the most honorable way that I could. I stood in this five-story building, all alone. I didn't know what to do during the day. The phone wasn't ringing. My marriage and the rest of my studio family was gone.

While I'd reached the highs of my career, I never imagined that I'd become millions in debt with an uncertain outlook on what would happen next. In a way, though, as I stood looking out onto Hell's Kitchen from my window, I realized I was still lucky to have myself and, albeit a gilded, roof over my head. Meanwhile, stories below me, millions of other families were struggling to make ends meet. Perhaps, they had kids to put through college, and they had lost all of their life savings. It reminded me that I came from more humble beginnings. This thought gave me some much needed perspective in a moment where I felt I'd lost everything.

I managed to go through a divorce, and then I got a buyer for the building that allowed me to pay off my debt to the bank and get out of that building and pay off some of the other debts that were surrounding me. However, that left me with almost nothing. I decided that I needed to start a new life now that my wife had left. My business had changed, but I had an opportunity to start all over in Los Angeles.

After many years commuting for work, I was just as comfortable in Los Angeles as I was in NYC. It felt like an opportunity to start anew and still maintain my world in Los Angeles, where I was well known as a photographer and where no one really knew my NYC problems. In a serendipitous bit of fate, I sold my building to the foundation of one of my photography heroes and mentors, the late Richard Avedon. I was moving on from something that I had created and that had once represented my image, but even in that transition, I managed to uphold my status in the photography world.

So I packed it all up – five floors worth of a life. I was still going back and forth to Los Angeles as I was planning my move. I managed to find a place to move into, and I found a small office as my new studio for the storage of my archive. I was literally working with such a small amount of funds, and Elizabeth supported it all. I remember the two of us having lunch together in that building before packing it all up just before the move. It went from this staff and all of these people to just the two of us, and I was depressed. I had lost my future. I'd lost my lifestyle, my wife, my business. It all was seemingly collapsing, yet I managed to keep it together and not go bankrupt and make sure that people got paid. I dealt with the stress of the enormity of a collapse of the world I knew. Elizabeth and I would sit there at lunch, and she would say to me, "God bless you. Just God bless you. You are an amazing man. You managed to deal with all of this pain and all of this stuff. You are such a big man. I've never met anybody like you. God bless you."

And so I packed up everything I had built along the way. Elizabeth was still working from her home in Brooklyn and managing what was left of my finances. While I was on one of my trips in LA, I met a beautiful woman who, for the first time since my marriage, caught my attention. Her name was Camie, and she had the brightest smile and energy. I met her through one of my clients, and I had never really met anyone like her before. I was enamored with her positive energy, something I desperately needed in my life with everything that happened. She had the greatest laugh and smile, and at that time, I really needed to laugh and have smiles.

I had left this event where she was working, and for the first time in my life, I walked back in and pulled myself together and went up to her and said, "I've never done this before, but I just think that you're amazing, and I would like to get to know you. Can I get your phone number?" She was warm and friendly and, yes, gave me her number. We kept in touch, and all of a sudden, we were something – we were dating. After 20 years of marriage, there was all of this newness and the beginning of a new relationship.

She became a fixture in the transition into my new life. She helped me with the move to Los Angeles and finding my new home and office. I even brought her to New York, and she got to see my building and see my world before I moved. The properties had been sold, and I decided to make this permanent transition to the West Coast. I finally settled into Los Angeles but still went back and forth, visiting my family and cleaning up all that was left in NY. I was juggling whatever jobs and whatever money was coming in and trying to cover my bills and expenses. Although everything had changed, some things now felt like they were changing for the better. All of a sudden, my work felt more exciting, more organic and spontaneous. I felt free despite all of the encumbrances that were placed on me leading up to this moment. Camie was beautiful, smart, and sexy, and she made me feel more youthful and loved. It all just started to feel like I had a future again, that it was all going to be okay.

On the day of my move to LA, it took two and a half tractor trailers to move all of the file cabinets, furniture, books, equipment – all of my things. Although I was trying to manage my expenses and keep the money coming in, the move to LA required a large one-time expenditure. However, I managed it. I managed it all thanks to Camie and the other woman in my life who was joining me in my LA adventure: Elizabeth.

Trying to continue to balance my financials, I developed a new relationship with a bank in Los Angeles. One day, my bank officer called me up. "Tim, could you come in a second?" he said. "I want to talk to you about a couple of things."

I went into his office.

"Tim, do you know who this guy is?" he asked.

I said, "No, that name doesn't sound familiar."

"Well, there's some checks that you wrote to him."

"What? No, I'm not familiar with who that is."

"Well, there are multiple checks for a certain amount of money, and that was a bit suspicious to me."

"Oh, that's interesting. No, I have no idea who that is."

So I looked a little deeper into my finances, and, of course, I asked Elizabeth what could be going on.

"What do you mean?" she said.

I had to get progressively clearer in what I was asking for, but I never got real answers.

Then, the next week, my bank officer called me back again, and he pointed out a number of other things. All of a sudden, I started to get a sick feeling, suspicious that there was money exchanging hands or going in and out of my bank account that I was not aware of. As we looked deeper, we found that through different means – checks written to people, checks made out to cash, as well as wire transfers – there were transactions I wasn't aware of, and we still didn't quite know what it was all for.

I'd given freedom to my bookkeeper because of our 20-year relationship, and because of the nature of my travels and everything else, all of my trust was in her. I just assumed, of course, that everything was fine; however, when I questioned her a bit more, she started to stumble even further in her comments. She admitted that those checks to that gentleman were to her landlord.

Stunned, I replied, "Well, why am I paying your landlord?"

The more this unfolded, the more we realized that she was freely using my bank account for her own personal means. Holding onto the adage of keeping your friends close and your enemies closer, I did not freak out on her but instead started to question. The more I questioned and the more I looked closer with my banker, I kept finding things that just didn't make sense to me. The more I talked to Elizabeth, the more she revealed. Eventually, she broke down and apologized, crying into the phone. Again, I managed my emotions so that I did not scare her away without finding out exactly what was going on. I then tried to get her to make an exchange by email, so I had some things in writing. She did answer and committed herself in some ways, but I still didn't quite know the scope of it. My bank suggested that I dig into this deeper and try to see the extent of what we think might have been going on.

I requested the records from my bank, and with the help of Camie, we sat around the pool on weekends and went through boxes and boxes of checks and bank statements. If she saw something that seemed to be a flag, she'd show it to me for my recognition and approval, or if I saw something that didn't make sense, I'd question her.

"What do you think?" I'd say. "Does this look like my signature? It sort of does, but maybe it's not."

The bank gave me the records from the previous eight years, and we started to find things: signatures that were clearly not mine but similar forgeries, checks made out to cash, wires made out for things that I had no idea what they were for. All of a sudden, a forensic picture was being drawn for me, and the picture was big. The more I dug into it, the more I realized that this had been going on for a long time. Over the eight year period, we found hundreds of thousands of dollars spent, but it still wasn't clear how much. I had known Elizabeth for 20 years, and she had such freedom. *When we were sitting together at lunch, was she secretly paying her landlord – and who knows what else – with my money?* Suddenly I questioned everything – again.

I then knew that my bookkeeper had somehow betrayed me. I wasn't quite sure yet of the scope, but following the dissolution of my marriage, my income being drastically reduced, the loss of employees and friends, my parents' difficulty in carrying on their life without our assistance, my problems with the NY bank and the legal issues that occurred from my properties and debt...well, it all just felt like too much to really face and accept. However, I had to take the burden on my shoulders and deal with what was in front of me. As the enormity of this betrayal affected me, I relied on my relationship with Camie and my new life in Los Angeles. There was so much that I had left behind that was really so painful, yet in some way, I rejected it. I pushed it down. I just didn't know how I could possibly deal with it all as they were such big, life changing issues that I couldn't face. But, in fact, that's not who I am, and I've always been the person who was able to carry a lot on my shoulders as I walked through the wall of fire...or so I thought. I made myself believe that, and I just kept walking and just kept dealing.

My relationship was a support. My friends were a support. My new life in Los Angeles, which seemed wide open and exciting, was a support. However, I guess I pushed down all that was on my shoulders...and I pushed it down...and I pushed it down...and now I look at it and feel like maybe I didn't really process it in some way. I made myself believe that I was processing it, but how could I? How could I just continue to take the hit and not have it affect me in some way? It's only now in retrospect that I feel it was just another betrayal and another issue and burden that has affected me and has kept me from dealing with things in my life a certain way.

On one hand, I was looking at myself and saying, *You're so strong. Look at all that you can deal with. You face everything. You're not afraid to address issues. You're not afraid to answer the questions. You're not afraid to look in the mirror. You're not afraid to look at what's happening around you and say that it doesn't really matter. What matters are the more important things in life. These are just the ups and the downs that come with not just a life in general but certainly a bigger life.*

...But it *definitely* affected me, and now I can see years later that it made me more protective. It made me less willing to trust people in relationships and just life in general. I always treated life like, as long as I trusted myself, I was fine, but in reality, trust is a much bigger word. It goes very deep, and I still struggle with all that trust means.

As I talked to my accountant and my lawyer and struggled with the enormity of the financial loss and how to move forward, we came to the conclusion that it was such a large amount of money and I so entrusted Elizabeth with my financial business, that, if I didn't go to the authorities with it, they might think that I was somehow in cahoots and that she and I were pulling some sort of fast numbers game and cooking the books, as it were.

My instinct was to not have any more pain. My instinct was to not deal with any more betrayal. My instinct was to just move forward and let it be. This woman was not going to give me satisfaction through justice being served or apologizing to me. I certainly wasn't going to get my money back, and I had tried my hardest to start a new life, to turn the page, to start another chapter. I didn't think this was going to help me move forward in life. It was just going to keep me down. It was the same thing, like my marriage. I didn't want to wallow in what was. I wanted to move on. Life is so short. I'm so consciously aware of it. And all of these things around me, especially my parents' last few years of their lives continually made me recognize time and how short everything is. That's always been my mindset: keep moving, keep moving, keep moving; stay in motion because that is how we get the most from life instead of reliving the anguish of the past.

However, the advice from my accountant and lawyer was, "If you don't do this, there could be an issue." So I thought about whom I would contact. Well, the police weren't going to do anything. Plus, I was in Los Angeles, not New York City anymore, and no one was going to do anything. Had a real crime taken place? And how could I prove that? Going to the FBI was even more far-fetched, so that made no sense. Therefore, I made a phone call to the District Attorney's office in Lower Manhattan. I got an assistant DA on the phone and told them the story, what I had discovered, and the whole relationship with my bookkeeper. They listened for quite a long time on the phone and then said that they would get back to me.

A number of days later, I got a phone call from the DA's office, explaining that the District Attorney wanted to meet with me and set up an appointment; they advised me to bring in my attorney with me. So, even though I was in Los Angeles, I made a plan. I set a calendar date with the DA's office in New York and flew east to meet with them in their offices in Lower Manhattan. I walked in the conference room, and there was the District Attorney with probably six other young people who seemed like junior lawyers or law clerks. They sat and listened to me as I went on with my story and told them everything. At the end of the story, I told them that I did not want to press charges, that, honestly, I was only there to make a record of what I had experienced, that I didn't expect any retribution or any compensation for what had taken place, and that I just wanted to move on. I said that this woman was not really a criminal in my mind and that she was just someone who got caught up in something or was desperate.

At that point, the District Attorney turned to me and said, "Although we respect your sentiment and realize that you're trying to do the right thing, this is out of your hands now and no longer about you and your case, but, in fact, this is a crime against the people of the state of New York. I need to do what I need to do to bring her to justice. She will be arrested, and we will need to move forward with a case against her."

I was emotional and a little agitated by that but accepted what had happened. I then asked the District Attorney if they needed anything from me; I could certainly supply any information or anything else they needed. He turned to me and said, "I'm the District Attorney. I don't need anything from you. I can get all the information that I need. She will be arrested, and you probably won't hear from us again."

I tried to move on and, again, accepted what was. A number of months later, I got a phone call, and it was from someone in the DA's office. They said, "Timothy, we... normally wouldn't do this, but we remember the way you felt about this situation, so we thought we'd let you know that she was arrested and that she was convicted of grand larceny."

I don't remember if they said she was going to serve time, but I remember they said that her passport would be taken away from her and that, in some way, she would have to deal with her punishment, though they did not elaborate.

The challenges that are placed in front of you in life often leave you with only one choice: accept that you are only in control of one thing – your attitude toward that which challenges you. This way of thinking is the only way to accept and move on. There's something I read all the time that says, if you think about a situation you worry about and you think about where you'll be one year, two years, five years from that point...more than likely the situation will not be there. If that is the case, don't let it control so much of your life.

This makes me realize so much about how we cannot control all that happens in our lives; instead, the only thing we can control is our attitude toward it. By attitude I mean our ability to face adversity in the moment and recognize that it's just a moment. I know that I'm still in motion, and my ability to stay in motion, until that time when I'm no longer, is what keeps me healthy, in mind and spirit, and allows me to be open to all that this life offers.

Chapter 20
Joseph Levy

My father was always sort of a private guy. As gregarious and funny and impish as he was, he was still somewhat quiet, in that he kept to himself and didn't say much about his personal life. Oh, he told us about his childhood and his parents who had died when he was young but never with any real details. His father died when he was 16, and his mother died when he was 20. Right after she passed, he was alone without any real family except an aunt and uncle in New York City whom he was not very close with. They were Park Ave wealthy and a world away from his upbringing in New Jersey. He joined the Navy right away, stayed for seven years during World War II and then came out and married my mother.

But I'm jumping ahead of myself.

He did talk about his parents, but I still don't feel that I know them. I grew up with my mother's side, the large Italian family from New Jersey, but never met my paternal grandparents, obviously, and didn't feel connected to that side of the family. There really wasn't another side, actually. My father always said he was Irish and talked about his mother and her last name, but we didn't know much of anything else. She was Irish

Catholic, a good woman, and her maiden name was Heaphy. He said she still had ties to the old country.

In the beginning of my photographic career, after college, around 1984, I went to Ireland on assignment and took my father with me as my assistant. We explored the pubs and landscape of Ireland as I took so many pictures, all with my dad's help. While there, we went to the parish where my father's family was from and tried to look up his birthrights, but to no avail. We never really talked about his father much. When we did talk about it, it always felt somewhat removed, almost like he wasn't around much in my father's life. My father talked about him as kind of a hustler and a gambler. I never really knew what he did. I don't remember ever being told what he did for a living, but he was always somehow hustling this or that. It's the impression that I got from my father, that he was sort of a street character, not a lowlife or criminal in any way, but someone who was always working some angle. My father had always said things about his dad that were sort of funny, even reverential, and always kind and with respect.

Yet again, there was always this sort of gambler or hustler kind of impression that I was given about his dad's life. At one point, my father said that when he was a teenager, his father had given him a tattoo kit. Now, I don't know what kind of parent gives their son a tattoo kit, but this was the early thirties, I assume, and my father talked about giving tattoos to the kids in the neighborhood. It was an odd thing to hear, but as a young child who was brought up close with my dad and with this feeling of street awareness and a sensibility toward something that was a bit irreverent, which certainly my father was, it seemed like an okay thing and something that fit right into my future sensibilities as an irreverent, alternative-minded teenager.

My father was born in 1919, which means that his memories of his father were certainly from the twenties and right into the early thirties. My father had lived through the Depression, the death of both of his parents, World War II, and whatever other trials and tribulations of his life that he faced as a young man. My father, in his quiet way, had mentioned that he had a sister who, as a one-year-old, somehow drank lye and died. This traumatized the family and, of course, my young father. Although he told me this tragic story, I never knew any real details about it because he didn't reveal them. *How did she get into the lye? Had she crawled into a kitchen cabinet? Where was the rest of the family?* He never told us exactly how he felt after his baby sister died or how this death occurred other than it did.

My father must have had a tough life, not having his dad around and then experiencing the tragedy of losing a sister, then being so young when he lost his father, and then, just a few years later, losing his mother, who seemed so dear to him just by the way he had always spoken of her. I remember, as a young boy, we used to go to the cemetery where my father's parents were buried. We visited maybe once a month. He and I would go, and we'd bring a lemon and wire brush that we used to scrape and scrub the bronze cemetery marker that represented the only part of that side of the family that I ever knew. I'll never forget these visits and the marker or the names on it.

It said "White" at the top and "Albert L." underneath with his mother, "May," next to it and the dates of their deaths below. I never knew what my grandfather's middle name was, even though it said "Albert L." on the grave marker. I always knew it was May Heaphy and, of course, Albert White, but I never knew the middle initial and what it meant. The cemetery was this enormous property, with very expansive acreage. I remember going regularly, and I actually liked the cemetery, partly I guess because it was something that my dad and I did together. There was something about it with its big stone, beautiful, ornate private mausoleums that were from very wealthy families. There was something about it all that really intrigued me. There was a separate enormous field where my father's parents were buried, which was a large sloping hill that looked out onto the rest of New Jersey, but on that big hill were hundreds, no, thousands of bronze markers that were just laying flat in the ground.

In that part of this cemetery, there were no headstones. There were no graves that were above ground at that section of the cemetery – it went on forever – but I always knew where to go. As we showed up in the cemetery and parked the car, I ran down to where my grandparents were buried. It was a regular and important thing that my father and I shared.

As I got older and started to go to another cemetery in Fort Lee where my mother's family was buried, in about four or five family plots, I noticed many differences. Some were headstones, some were those bronze markers that lay flat on the ground, but in any case, it became a regular thing to go to the cemetery with my folks. It was an outing that I did with my parents to go and visit family members. There was something about the cemetery that always made me feel comfortable, and it always made me feel like I had a connection to all of those family members who were gone, even though I was so young and knew so few of them.

As my parents got older and very much into their nineties, whenever I was back home from LA and trying to help take care of them later in their life, I would take them on trips to the cemetery. I would put them in the car, and we'd go for a ride because that was all we could really do as they did not have the energy or the physical capability of doing many other things. That was always an important part of our outings, something that I knew I was doing for them that was special and gave them a connection to their past and something that had always been a part of our collective outings and collective connection to family. In fact, to this day, whenever I head back to the East Coast, one of the first things I do is go to the cemetery and visit with family members, always by myself, always feeling comfortable and always talking to them, praying, if you will, and still having that connection that stemmed from childhood.

As a boy, I would anxiously go to the other cemetery where my father's parents were buried, which was called Fairview Cemetery in Fairview, NJ, and my mother's family cemetery, the Madonna Cemetery in Fort Lee, a couple of towns over. I would go to the Fairview Cemetery with my father. It was very important, just a father-son outing, even though he did bring my mother and sisters there during certain holidays when we would always make a point to visit family on those special days. I would always think of that aged cemetery as something from another period of time, as something from part of our history that I feel connected to, relative to family and time. I've always felt so connected to that period, the forties, and then of course the fifties and the sixties when I grew up. In the seventies, when I became a teenager and got a little more distant from that part of my family dynamic, I still visited the cemeteries, and, actually, as I delivered for a florist in high school, I was often at both places making flower deliveries. No matter what I was doing, the cemetery always represented something that I needed to respect, needed to go back to and needed to visit. I was connected somehow. I don't know how; I don't know why; but I still, to this day, feel a strong but comfortable connection to my family history through the cemetery. When my parents got older, and certainly as my father started to age quickly after the heart attack and the bypass surgery that he endured, he started to get dementia, and in that dementia, he would repeat stories, as many people as they get older do. It was interesting to watch, and as I visited my family more and came back into the fold after the intensity of my career and my self-involved, focused time spent on building my own life and family and profession, I would sit with my parents in their home in Fort Lee and simply listen to them. My mother would go off as usual, talking about herself and about the things that bothered her, but my father would tell stories and say things that would be surprising. I'd feel like all of a sudden I was hearing things that I hadn't heard before.

Again, my father was somewhat quiet about his past, except for those major facts about his life, his father, his mother, briefly about his sister, and then, of course, about the Navy and his experiences there and how important the Navy was to him in that part of his life. It makes sense. He was 20; it was his first time alone and out in the world after his parents had passed. He was experiencing not just the travels of the world and what that does but also the camaraderie and the work ethic and everything that comes with being in the military. He was also on a ship, and it was during the most immense war of our history. So that part of his life was big, and we heard those stories throughout our lives growing up. But in those, perhaps unfiltered, moments, as he began to slip into dementia, there were other things that he started to share.

When you get older, it seems you can't remember what you have for lunch, but you certainly start to talk about things from your past that come up from deep inside the file cabinets of your mind. The memories from childhood and other times in your life come up and are sometimes revelatory because they can be things you never said or that your family has not heard before. In my father's case, that's when he told me about his father buying him a tattoo kit and all these different interesting things about his family. However, there was one thing that we never really talked about, and that was really what his father and his mother were like or what their relationship was like or how they met or what their parents, my grandparents, were like or their backgrounds. That was something that I just never knew, and it seemed that it was so long ago and, because my father's parents died, that then maybe we'd never hear it. Unfortunately, at some point, his dementia got worse, and what he said started to become babble. That was sad, but there was also still humor in it. My father always had humor in who he was.

Then that babble turned into almost nothing; he couldn't communicate anymore. He was still strong as an ox; he was just a strong, strong man. I respect him so much to this day and always did, even as a young boy, but he became a strong guy who couldn't speak any longer. We were taking care of him in a way that we felt best, even though the majority of what one would consider a quality of life was gone. We continued to give him a protected and well-cared-for life to the end. During this time, as quickly as she was changing too, my mother acted as if my father was okay; I guess, in her mind, he just changed. That's all. It felt like she almost pretended, or maybe she didn't really see it clearly, due to her own age and oncoming dementia, that he really had become something completely different...so much less than he was.

In any case, at that point, we started to take care of his affairs. My parents needed help. They were in their late nineties, and my mother never did much of anything for herself and was never capable of even keeping a checkbook. My father did everything, took care of all the family business, and took care of my mother. Therefore, it was time for us to take charge and take care of them. With me living in a different place, and being the youngest in the family, it fell to my eldest sister, Mary, who was more administratively oriented and had the capability, with her husband being an attorney, to take on this new role. Maybe just because of her position in the family in terms of her age, it seemed like her job to take this on, and as she did and started going through my father's office and going through his papers and trying to not only get a handle on how to maintain and run their lives in their present forms but also understand their history, their insurance, their cemetery plot that was going to be used imminently and all of the other things that were necessary for their elder care.

Mary called me one day.

"I've got to talk to you," she said. "I found something."

Although I don't remember how it was said, I certainly recognized the importance of what she was saying through the tone of her voice. She told me how she found a piece of paper that was so "strange," that my father had a legal name change in 1936 when his father had died. Apparently, his mother went to court and had his name changed legally from Levy to White. *What does that mean?! What?!* I just didn't know what to say. My father's last name was not White, it was Levy. He didn't tell us. He was 16 years old in 1936, or maybe 17.

How could he not know?

Of course, he knew and never told us and, seemingly, never told my mother either. No one ever knew my father kept a secret his whole life, from the time he was a teenager to this day in his nineties. We're talking 80 years! *He had no idea that it was important to tell his children such a story? How could he not? How could it not be important? He wasn't six years old; he was 16. How could he not feel that this was an important thing to share? How could we not know the history? How could it not have come up? How could it not be part of his personal history, his personal story? How could it not have come up in different areas as we grew up and learned about our parents and their family's past?* All we ever knew was that my father's parents died when he was young. All we ever knew was that he was alone after that. All we ever knew was that he joined the Navy and then came out and married my mother. It's almost as if life started from that point forward, this new family that my father had taken on, my mother's family and his own new family and children. We were shocked. My sister and I didn't quite know what to do, but we both decided that it was now our secret.

Why continue to keep the secret? Mary and I wanted to break the news once we had all the information at hand. Initially, we didn't quite understand what we had just discovered, even though it was clear that it was a legal document and that something dramatic had happened in our family history. Not long after this discovery, Mary and I talked and thought... *Wait a minute... Levy...Our last name was Levy, and now it's White? What does this mean?* Then my sister Mary called again to say she had gotten a letter from Fairview Cemetery where my father's parents were buried, and it said something to the effect of a renewal or something on the lease on the grave. It mentioned Albert Levy, and, again, it started to finally make sense to us that my father's father was not named Albert White...His name was Albert Levy...and we knew nothing about this.

All of a sudden, the middle initial on the grave made sense. It wasn't Albert L. White, it was Albert L....Albert Levy...and May White, yet the heading on the grave was White. *Why?* Because my father buried them there, and he made the decision on how the grave was marked. When the cemetery got in touch with my sister, they initially mentioned Levy, which threw her off. Apparently, the cemetery knew his last name, but we never did. My father never told us. He clearly never told my mother, who just didn't know, because if she did know, she would never have been able to keep that kind of a secret. That's not who she was. *But why all of this, why would he have kept a secret from her, from us, from the world?* It didn't make sense. Mary and I decided to break the news to the rest of the family, including Jamie, once we had all the facts of the situation. We also wanted to reveal our father's secret in the most dignified manner possible. When we told Jamie and the family, it was a relief for my father's yearslong secret to be fully out in the open. The hidden story had now become a knowable part of our familial lore.

My whole life was about understanding the background, the history behind something, the importance of history, and certainly family history. It was the thing that really got me started in photography, which was this sense of family and the photographic images that represented it to me. I went to the library – this was before the ease of our reliance on Google and the internet – and started looking things up. I found birth records in New York, and I found my father, which took me to his parents, which took me to the precise truth about my grandfather's, *my father's father's*, last name being Levy. He was Albert Levy; he was from Germany. My grandmother's name was May Heaphy, and she was from Ireland. They had come to this country and had two children, Joseph and his sister Margarette, who died when she was one.

All of a sudden, I had truth. All of a sudden, I had history. There was very little information, but I had something. I had the true answer that this really was our family story, that my father's father's name was Levy. That means my father's real name is Levy. That means my name is Levy. *What the fuck? This is a story.* I reveled in the fact that my father, who decided to keep a secret his whole life, now with dementia, could not tell us the truth.

*Oh, the irony of it all! Oh my God, this story is such an interesting part of our family history? What a script. I just discovered what I believe is an odd personal story that should be told, that should be written down, that should be somehow shared with others. It's so unique. How do you tell anybody? We couldn't even tell my sister. My mother doesn't know. No one knows, but Mary and I...*So we kept it to ourselves for a bit.

Later, we told my sister Jamie. She reacted in such shock and was definitely offended by it. She was offended that my father didn't tell her the truth. She was offended that she didn't have all the answers and or know her family history. She felt slighted, as if she didn't know herself in some way. In any case, she reacted strongly, even made comments relative to the blood disease sickle cell anemia in Black people and the one prevalent in Ashkenazi Jews.

"Well, is this going to affect my children and their children's health?" she said. "Is this going to affect my personal life and heritage?"

It's so interesting how we all related to this revelation about our family. I reveled in the fact that my father kept a secret his whole life, that we only uncovered it after he couldn't speak or address it or tell us the real answers or the reasons or the whys or what he felt during his life.

I thought it was so brilliant.

Mary, also interested in family and family history, just thought it was a unique approach to the understanding of who we are. She also loved my father so much and felt, I think, some closeness to him that came from this, something that was her secret with him. Being the eldest and the one who found this information first, I think it was something that she owned, but I also think she and I both felt it was such a funny, interesting, laughable, yet seriously strange part of our family history. She shared it with her husband, of course. He and I were always close, so we now had this sort of joke about our family and how wacky they all were. Now the joke just got bigger and stronger and funnier.

Well, all of a sudden, I started to think about the tattoo that was on my father's arm, which I always thought was an anchor. It was actually these strange little marks that were like a J and a L, and they were back against each other, which formed what could be interpreted as the shape of an anchor. *Why?* Because as a child my father always told me he had gotten that tattoo when he was in the Navy, and the Navy was such an important part of his life. He talked about that all of the time. As a boy, I thought it was like Popeye, who had an anchor tattoo. Then one day, it hit me: the connection with my father telling that story of his father giving him a tattoo kit and the nature of that tattoo on his arm and how unfinished it was, how simple it was. It wasn't really an anchor! If it were an anchor, it would look like an anchor. *Duh.* Instead, it was these two letters, these two little marks: they were a J and an L.

They were his initials. My father's father had given him a tattoo kit as a young teenager, maybe exactly around the time that he passed away, and he put those initials on his arm to honor something. You could see it was rough. It was a handmade tattoo. It was off center, and it was on his left forearm. It was a J, and it was an L. It struck me so poignantly that he had made a gesture to put his initials on his arm, about the things that he lost, which was who he was. Joseph Levy was no longer Joseph Levy. He was Joseph White, and he needed to, in some way, carry on a new identity. He put those initials on his arm in a tattoo forever to honor his father and his name, Joseph Levy: *JL*. It made total sense. After seeing and talking about this tattoo my whole life with my father, it finally made sense.

Then I started to think about why the name change, why the secretiveness of it. Then I thought about it and came to a conclusion. It was 1936 when his father died. It was a time when fascism was rampant in the world, when Nazism was on the rise, when Jews were being persecuted in Germany and around the world, and my father's father was German. *Wait a minute, are we Jewish? What? I've been brought up Catholic my whole life. I've been told I was Irish. I was an Irish Italian Catholic my whole life. All of a sudden, now I'm a Jew?* Well, not really because, of course, it's your mother that carries on the religion in the Jewish faith, not your father, but still. My grandfather was Jewish, a German Jew. Well, all of a sudden it started to make sense that my father's mother was left alone in 1936 when all of this horror was happening in the world. She was left alone with a child, a single mom with the last name Levy, a German Jew.

Now, *that's* scary.

She must've been scared to death, and so she changed their names, a legal name change in the courts in New Jersey to White. She picked the most Aryan name possible, it seems. She changed his name to Joseph White, and for some reason she impressed upon him the secretive nature of this and why it should be kept a secret...because he did. He went into the war. He went into the Navy during World War II, which was being fought against the Nazis, the persecutors of the Jews. He lived it. *Why did he keep this a secret his whole life?* I will never know, but from the information, the mark on his arm, the stories and the legal documentation of this name change...I can only assume that I'm correct in what I feel, and that's all I know. There were no living relatives. There was no one to tell the story. It was a long time ago. It's almost impossible to know for sure because we have such little information that my father gave us, other than the name and the name change.

It's all I know about my father's family, my family prior to my father. So we lived with this for a couple of years as my father hung on to life. Unable to speak, having full elder care, moving in with my sister, who took in both of my parents into their nineties, into her home, he *must* have felt loved as we sat, and we looked at him, and we took care of him, and we loved him...and we loved his wife, and we took care of her as they both approached a hundred years old. Knowing this secret, knowing this story, but not fully understanding, we made jokes of it. We laughed, but there's something deep here for me. There was something deep about family history that really struck me and really was an important part of this man who meant so much to me, who means so much to me.

The connection that we had, the strength with which he brought me up, the strength he gave me as a man, the integrity, the pride, the sense of self that my father gave to me, his humor, his sense of rough, tough street smarts, and yet balanced with a soft gentleness that made up who my father was – made me who I am; I see that now. His character, his influence informed my personality and was a very important part of who I had become.

This stayed with me until the day my father died. After seeing his body and giving it over to the undertakers, I drove into New York City and found a tattoo artist. I had a picture of my father's arm that I had taken years earlier at my father's house when I asked him to pose for me. I took a picture of his arm because I knew it was important. I knew that tattoo meant something before I got any of this information because we had talked about it and it was a conscious mark on my father.

Again, his tattoo represented something that was streetwise about him, something about my dad, that rougher side of him that I never quite knew the truth about. I sensed the tattoo meant something, and I'd photographed it. So I had it with me, and I went to that tattoo artist the day of my father's death and said, "I want this tattoo put on my arm, and it's got to look handmade, and it's got to look off center, and it's got to look like it's an eighty-year-old faded tattoo just like it did on my father's arm. It's got to be exactly like this picture."

The tattoo artist said, "Oh, yeah, I got it."

Forcefully, I said, "No, you don't get it. It needs to be exactly like this."

I cried as the ink became a permanent part of me. I now wear my father's tattoo on my arm like a badge of honor. Although it may not have been the Navy-inspired "anchor" I thought it was for most of my life, it grounded me all the same.

I wear that tattoo as the piece of my family history and my father's history that I will carry with me to the day I die.

Chapter 21
Speaking of Death

At 6:00 a.m. one morning, I got a phone call from my brother-in-law, Dennis.

My father had passed.

They were the words no one wants to hear, though I knew they had been a whisper away for a long time. I had prepared for the day for a while, feeling a strong sense of responsibility to my family and myself during what we knew were my father's last years. The feeling in my heart, instead of sadness or fright, was acceptance...acceptance that, perhaps now, dad could really rest in peace.

When I got off the phone with Dennis, I called my travel agent, John Wing, and told him I needed to get on the absolute next plane to New York. Quickly, I threw together a few shirts, pants, and, of course, my camera into a bag, sped to the airport, parked my car, and ran to my gate. I also called my friend Chaps to let him know that Chief Petty Officer White had passed. On the flight, I started to write his eulogy. Through my scribbled words on a notebook, I wanted to honor the masculinity and strength that I always saw in my dad. Although the last few years saw him bedridden,

I wanted to honor the strong, capable man he was throughout most of his life.

My flight didn't arrive in New York until 8 p.m., a full 14 hours after Dennis had called me with the news. From JFK Airport, a car service took me across Manhattan, all the way into New Jersey.

As I entered my sister's house around 10:00 p.m., I braced myself for what I might see, as I'd already made one request of her before flying over: to keep my father in his bed and to wait for me while I traveled from LA. I wanted to see him in his last moments and to have my own time with him. As his chief caretaker, my sister had a hospital bed for him in her living room, where my dad laid immobile for the past few years. On the first floor, it was easier for my sister and his other caregivers to be there for him, so they had likely been walking around his body just laying there in bed, in her living room, for those 14 hours I was traveling. It had to have been a hard thing to ask them to do – odd, perhaps selfish, even – but at the time, I was insistent.

From the darkened porch, lit by only two small lights, to the low lamp light inside of my sister's home, I finally saw my whole family waiting as I walked in. They had been waiting to call the funeral home to pick up the body and somehow endured the daylong wait that I had requested. It was actually kind of eerie. Everyone was standing or sitting in different, separate positions around the room, around one central figure: my father, whose body was lying in bed just as they had found him that morning. My mother was sitting in the chair to the left. No one really said hello, just nodded; in fact, no one said anything. It was silent. I walked in and went right to my mother and knelt in front of her.

"Dad's gone, Mom, but he's in heaven now," I said, grabbing her hand to help her out of her chair. "Let's all say goodbye to him." I held her arm as we went to his bedside. Laying my head on him, I just held his hands and whispered, "I love you, dad," all the while making sure I didn't ignore

Mom. We said goodbye together, at least that's what I was attempting to do.

Then, something came over me: I recognized how selfish I'd been, making everyone wait for those 14 hours while I arrived to say my goodbye, as if my farewell was more of a priority than theirs. It snapped me right out of a trance, in a way. I stood up, turned to my sisters, and said it was time to call the funeral home. Forty-five minutes later, the funeral home van arrived in our driveway. They wrapped him in a white sheet and body bag, laid him on a metal gurney, and placed him in the vehicle.

The room completely changed. I could see the peace on each person's face.

The responsibility was over.

The day of death was over.

That night, I stayed at Whoopi's house, about a mile or so away from my sister's house, where I stayed every month for the past few years when I came to visit my father. She and I had spoken earlier, and she had given her condolences and acknowledged that I would show up to stay at her home sometime that evening.

The next morning, preparation and arrangements for his burial began. I picked up my sisters, and we went to the funeral home together. On the ride, we started to talk about how we would approach this meeting. I brought up a book I had read called *Smoke Gets in Your Eyes* by Caitlin Doughty, this goth chick who got a job in college at a crematorium and then eventually became a funeral director. In her book, she told the truth about the funeral industry and what goes on with embalming, how they basically put a fucking vacuum in your system, suck your guts out, and do what's necessary to make a body presentable for viewing. They basically abuse your body to put it into a state that is false and made up in an unnatural way for presentation at the funeral.

I had a really strong feeling about how to treat my father after death. He was so well taken care of by us and by his caregivers during the last few years of his life, so much so that when he was in the hospital with different issues in the months prior to his death, the nurses couldn't believe that he'd been in bed for a year and a half. "He's got no bed sores!" they'd say. Even in death, his body looked so good: his skin was supple, nails were clean, hair brushed, face shaved. Although he was bedridden and unable to move, speak, or feed himself, the caregivers made sure he was adjusted and comfortable throughout and flipped him over a number of times a day. The way he was taken care of was just beautiful.

The funeral director showed us into his office with an old glass-topped desk and a few nondescript chairs. This particular funeral home was the same one where my father buried his mother in 1940. I found it so poignant that we brought him back there, but I still disagreed with how funeral homes in general prepared and embalmed bodies. In front of my sisters, I confronted the funeral director who was related to the owners of the funeral home, who may even have been involved in my grandmother's funeral. I asked about the reality of how the prep process for a body is handled, based on the book I'd read. But I also had this childhood interest in the funeral business and actually thought I'd wanted to be a mortician earlier in my life. Books on the subject fascinated me for years, even though I never actually entered the industry.

"Listen, I don't want to embalm him and put him up there on display in a casket. We took care of this man so fucking well for the last however-many years, and you're going to tear him apart and slap makeup on him and put him in a box and put him on display. That's not Joe White. He was a selfless, natural guy, and that's not the way we took care of him. Now you're going to abuse this body and make it plastic and put it on display? No. I say we cremate him."

My parents never put in writing their exact wishes for burial. My sisters were not prepared for my statement and didn't know I was going to say all of this. I turned to them and said, "Cremation is a cleaner, a better way that his molecules enter into the earth, allowing his ashes back into the atmosphere."

I turned back to the funeral director. "Am I right? You tell my sisters what you do. You basically abuse his body and suck at his guts. You staple his eyelids; you put plastic and whatever is necessary to do what you do to prepare a body. Tell them. Am I right?"

The funeral director, stunned, could only nod. "Yes, he's technically right."

"Here's my plan: we cremate him, put a casket up there at the funeral home and make everybody think that we're continuing in the Italian-Catholic tradition, that we're having a funeral and putting him on display. Instead of doing what we traditionally would do, we cremate him, and we put his ashes in the box. No one but us would know."

Although still a bit shocked, my sisters heard what I said and were not saying no. I was pretty powerful about it. Not that I wouldn't have accepted their rebuttal, but I thought, "Why not?"

And we agreed to do it as I suggested. Surprisingly, the funeral director agreed to do it too. It was official: my father's funeral would be a ruse. Funeral goers would think he was in the box, but it would only be his ashes.

After the funeral home, I took my sisters for a ride around where we grew up. We talked about Dad, how funny and quirky he was, little stories from childhood. For lunch, I took them to Hirams, a local hot dog stand from the 1930s near where we grew up that I used to take my father all the time. At first, Jamie refused because I guess she thought it was not serious enough. Mary, even though she's a vegetarian, came in and had a hot dog with me in the name of my father.

Our next stop was the church to meet with the priest and set up the mass for my dad...well, my dad's ashes. Sitting in the parking lot, in front of this holy building, the three of us never felt younger as we laughed our heads off, partly out of relief, partly from the absurdity of what we were doing. We were about to lie to a priest and then to everyone in the family at the funeral to come. If we even believed in it, we were all definitely going to hell, we joked, but, ultimately, we all seemed okay with it.

At the church rectory, we spoke with the priest about setting up the whole mass and the whole Catholic thing. When the day of the funeral came around, people were like, "Well, why is it a closed casket?" And we were like, "He didn't look so good at the end. We felt it better to present him as we remembered him." But the truth is, we just bought a box and convinced everyone that he was in it. We had him in an urn, and we lied about the whole thing.

The next day at his funeral, the only people who knew the truth were Dennis, Mary, Jamie, and me. However, the day itself would be an accurate representation of who my father was: incredibly self-effacing with a disarming sense of humor – oh, and, of course, his love for horse racing and secretly driving to the track to indulge in his biggest vice, gambling. All of these qualities cut the somber tone of the day and pointed to all signs that my father was pulling our funny bones from the Great Beyond. During the funeral mass, the priest encouraged funeral goers to shut their phones off. Nonetheless, during the mass, somebody's phone rang and their ringtone was *Call to the Post*, the bugle call that is played before a horse race. I remember being in the front row of the church with my family all lined up next to me in the pew, and I looked behind everyone and over to Dennis incredulously. He bent back and we looked at each other like, *What the fuck?! Who's ringtone would be that obscure tune?* It was too freaky. Everyone in the church chuckled. We were reminded that Joe White lived a long, healthy life, and that although we were grieving, we had a good feeling about who he was and what he left us with.

My friend Chaps, the naval chaplain whom I befriended a few years prior, had flown in from Norfolk to be with us and pay his respects. He actually stood by that whole week as we prepped for the funeral and shared our grief. This wonderful man, who so respected my dad and the naval tradition, made sure that my father had military honors at his burial. There was a sailor playing taps and another folding the American flag and presenting it to my mother. None of that would have ever happened if it weren't for Chaps' reverence for my dad and his service in the Navy. I remember my mother was in a wheelchair at the cemetery, and I wheeled her up a hill on the grass next to the grave site. The whole thing about the bugler and the sailors handing her the flag was really moving. It was a very small thing with only a handful of people at the gravesite, but it made such an impression and a dignified send off for my dad.

Chapter 22
Mom

In early May 2021, my sister Mary called to tell me our 101-year-old mom, who had been suffering from dementia for years, stopped eating. She asked me if she should take Mom to the hospital. Given my experience with my father and his dementia, I knew the experience could be not only potentially frightening, or at the very least disorienting for someone who was losing her mental capabilities, but also unlikely to help her live longer. After the phone call, I sat at my desk, paralyzed about what I should do next. That's when I called my dear friend Whoopi and asked for her guidance. It was comforting to feel that after many years of photographing her and being longtime friends who regularly kept in touch, she was there for me as much as I had been for her behind the lens.

She only had a few words for me: "You know what to do."

Then she hung up.

I packed a bag and rushed to the airport to get on the first flight to New York. When I arrived, I took a car to my sister's home in New Jersey. Both of my sisters were relieved to see me. Then I walked into my mother's room and sat right beside her. When she passed two hours later on May 8,

2021, I was kneeling in front of her next to the bed. I held her hand and felt present in her transition from life into death. I told my sisters I felt her go, and their emotional pain enveloped the house. I just knelt there in silence holding her hand and focused on what I had just felt. I closed my eyes and was so present in the moment. I deeply focused on my mom and our lives together. My mind created a slideshow of imagery, a flip book of memories from as young an age as I could remember, from childhood to present day: me as a little boy, a pre-adolescent, a teenager, a college student, a graduate, a man and me as I am today. Some of those memories were photo memories, things that stayed in my mind not because I remembered them directly but because I recalled from photos I saw growing up. As my mom left this plane, I sped through memory after memory like a flipbook. When I opened my eyes, I had tears running down my face...and I was at peace.

The funny hook to this story is that when my mother died five or six years after my dad, there was a whole other twist, similar to my father's. When she died, it was the middle of Covid, and because of all the deaths and the restrictions to business and public get-togethers, it was difficult to organize a funeral. They picked up her body but couldn't do anything with it, so they put her on ice. We wanted to do the same thing as my dad, as it seemed to make sense, but they wouldn't cremate her. Because of Covid, there were significant delays in the process. The church also wouldn't give us a mass in a reasonable amount of time because everything was delayed or canceled at that time. And then, even planning to do a repast afterward, which is a post-service gathering, no one would do it because no one was gathering in public places anymore. And so it went on. It was like a week or two after my mother died, and everybody seemed to express, "Can we pay our respects already? When will there be a funeral?" It was a we-want-to-get-this-done-and-put-her-to-rest kind of thing. So, my sisters and I got together and said, "Well, you know what? We're going to fake it again."

The funeral home had her on ice; they wouldn't cremate her because they were backlogged with all these Covid deaths; and they couldn't get a funeral date planned either.

"I've got an idea," I said to the funeral director.

"Let's do the mass. We can get a date from the church for next week. There won't be an actual funeral. Give me an urn."

I continued on to tell him that we'd bring the urn into church and carry it to the altar as we would have a casket. We'll pretend she's in the urn, even though she's not. Thus, for both my parents, we actually faked their funerals. I literally walked down the aisle with my niece, Molly, and a couple of other family members walking in unison as in a funeral mass procession. I held the urn, holding it as if my mother was in it. We had this formal mass, and we all spoke, as if she was there...even though she was still on ice in the funeral home. Afterwards, we found a restaurant that would allow us to finally have a repast, and people showed up, and we did the whole thing. It was done.

Weeks later, they finally burned her and sent us her ashes. We then buried her in the grave along with my father. Oh, that was the other thing: it was winter; the ground was frozen; and the cemetery burials were all backlogged as well. So we had to wait for months and months before they could put my mother in the ground with my father. The whole thing just became farcical but felt in line with all our strange family sense of humor. We knew my father was laughing throughout the whole thing, and for sure my mother was bitching.

Chapter 23
Cherry Blossoms

Undereye bags run in my family. Like a badge of honor, they appear around the eyes of every family member of a certain vintage in old photos. For many years, I thought this familial trait might skip a generation with me. I always worked to look my best, especially in my chosen career; plus, I was living in looks-conscious Beverly Hills, where youth, or at least a fresh appearance, seemed as necessary as air to breathe or iced coffee to drink in the morning.

However, that's not why I decided to get an eye job. A few years prior, my doctor did a biopsy for skin cancer under my left eye that left a tear-shaped divot on my face. I was glad I didn't have melanoma, but I was left staring at that small scar under my eye whenever I passed my own reflection. It was an unwelcome mark that seemed to wave back at me from the mirror.

Then I watched an interview of myself talking about my work, and I couldn't look away from the bags and the divot. *Did I need surgery?*

I made an appointment with a plastic surgeon I had met through a friend to go over my options. The doctor said he could fix the divot, but it would affect the same space under my eye and would essentially be a lift. I talked with him about the family bag situation, and he said that, given I wanted him to fix the left eye, he should do both. He said, by fixing more than the divot, it would correct my vain concerns. He said it would freshen me up.

"If you do one eye, you might as well do both," the doctor said.

Why not? It all sounded good and minimally painless. My healthy eating with virtually no slip-ups and working out six days a week in the gym may have done wonders for my body and mind, but the divot could only go via surgery. It was akin to someone getting a nose job after correcting a deviated septum. It wasn't all vanity; it was for health too. *Yeah, right.*

The procedure involved the doctor cutting inside my eyelid and pushing the fat down inside my skull, de-bagging my eye from inside out. He also took fat from my hips and injected it all over my face, neck and head to stimulate stem cell growth in a system called Mist – a bubbling fountain of youth for my face. *Wow.* This was much more than removing a divot. Because the fat would come from my hips, I was also technically getting lipo – a two for one I didn't consider before the divot became my new unwanted roommate.

On a warm spring afternoon, just a few days before my surgery was scheduled, I made an emergency visit to a retina specialist. I'd been experiencing painful, throbbing headaches. My vision became blurry. Floaters were appearing in my line of vision, which I learned was actually blood. The fear was that my retina had torn. No divot surgery could happen without knowing what was behind the pain and blurry vision.

My seventy-something-year-old doctor, a Beverly Hills retina specialist, entered the room and did an examination where he looked behind my eye. He put a prism-like loupe inside of my eye, and it reflected back all of the dimensions inside the back of my eyeball. Then he looked back at me and said he had found the issue: my retina had detached from my eye as part of a "natural" aging process. The doctor confirmed I couldn't go through with the divot surgery until I underwent a laser procedure to reattach my retina.

"How did this happen?" I asked. I had always taken good care of my eyes. They were the reason for my livelihood for over 30 years.

The doctor shrugged. "It could be for a multitude of reasons, but essentially it's an aging process that can happen to us all." The separation is natural; the fear is a tear.

My eye job was postponed until they could reconnect the retina and stop the bleeding. I had been prepping for the eye surgery for weeks with appointments with my general practitioner to make sure I was healthy enough for surgery: from Covid tests to pre-op medication and a whole lot of post-operative care instruction. Apparently, the eye job was a bigger deal than I thought, but for now, there was a more serious concern. The retina doc needed to perform a laser surgery to stop the separation and needed to do it immediately. I was ushered into his laser room and proceeded to have one of the most painful medical surprises I had ever experienced.

Afterward, I could barely see. I was told to rest my eyes over the weekend and not do anything that would strain them – no TV, no computer, no light. Everything, including opening my refrigerator door, was a bright, painful process. I came back to the office on Monday to see how I was improving but was told that I was still bleeding a lot behind my eye and that he needed to go back in with the laser to try to fix it. The ensuing two more laser surgeries over the next few days felt like two exquisitely precise, well, lasers doing a show in my skull. The pain was unbearable, and I was seriously worried. Here I was thinking about a cosmetic surgery when I was now undergoing three corrective ones. *Should I even go through with this eye job? What if I was giving myself even more serious sight issues?*

A month of healing and low-light resting later, I got a sign-off from the retina doc. He wasn't happy that I was going back in for another different eye surgery, but I had built this up and convinced myself that this was something I really wanted to do. The surgery was planned for a month later, and I started my week-long prep all over again.

My surgery was scheduled for 7 a.m. on a Monday.

"How are you getting here?" the nurse asked.

"Don't worry about it," I said. "I'll get there."

It was my grown-up version of what I said to my mother when I wanted to walk myself into kindergarten, "Mom, I've got this." She had watched me march into school with confidence I never knew I had until I tried it on that afternoon. I carried that same confidence with me that morning around 5 a.m., when I decided no one was going to drive me to the hospital. I'd walk.

Around 5 a.m. on a Monday morning, I threw on my sweats, grabbed my keys, and hiked six miles to the hospital. The sunrise was beautiful, my visual guide as I listened to an audio meditation on my earbuds. Each positive reinforcement I heard propelled me further and further down the road. I lived up in Coldwater Canyon, and at that hour, the main road was empty before the morning commuters. I walked in the middle of the road, lost in my thoughts and feeling the physical and mental change I was about to undergo.

Once I arrived, the nurse at the desk looked me over suspiciously. Maybe it was the copious amounts of sweat dripping down my shirt. I filled out some forms, and she again was worried about my transportation, this time who would pick me up and who was going to spend the night with me after I was let out of the hospital.

"What's the big deal...I'll be fine. We'll figure it out," I replied.

She said that answer wouldn't do; they would not even bring me into the operating room without knowing that I had someone taking me home and staying with me. I told her that my girlfriend was picking me up, and that, if not her, I would find someone else to stay with me at home if necessary. The nurse was not happy. She pursed her lips. If her eyes had been a buzzer, it would have been making a low "bahhh" sound, indicating I'd given an incorrect answer to the game show host. Realizing I did not have a plan, without telling me, she made arrangements for me to be transported into aftercare, a hotel for post-surgery patients to receive 24-hour care from a dedicated nurse, another very Beverly-Hills accommodation, though I wasn't trying to be a VIP. I was trying not to ask for help.

In my aftercare room, I woke up many hours later after the general anesthesia wore off. A thick gauze bandage was wrapped around my eyes, puffy from undergoing surgery. I could open my eyes, but I didn't want to since they were now super sensitive to light and movement. It was disorienting.

Seated in an elevated position in bed, I finally realized I wasn't alone: I inhaled the perfume of my new girlfriend at the time, who held me tight. The long blonde strands of her hair cascaded over my chest, and she told me everything was going to be OK. This was a new relationship, and I was so pleased when I openly told her of my surgery and how supportive she was.

"How did you find me?" I said, having done my best to have major surgery without alerting anyone, even the new, exciting love in my life. I expected her to pick me up after surgery and that I would be home in my bed. However, when I woke up in aftercare, disoriented from anesthesia and in a strange bed, it felt so good to have someone I cared so much about resting in my arms.

A few hours later, I heard footsteps at my door, a knock, and then the familiar voice of my house manager Adriana. For years, she took care of my home and life when I worked and traveled for most days of the year. She wasn't a housekeeper; she hired the housekeeper. If my gutters or windows needed cleaning, she found the expert to do the job. Every Saturday, she placed elaborate flower arrangements in every room of my house. She would always place large branches of cherry blossoms in my home because she knew how much I loved them. She had never met my girlfriend but gave me a supportive, pleasing look that let me know she approved. I love her and consider her a thoughtful and caring friend, and having her in my life made it feel like family.

The doctor's orders were to stay in aftercare for two days so I could heal. When the sun rose the next day, Tuesday, I was ready to bust out. The nurse tried to help me stand up, but I was too stubborn and wanted to do so on my own, even if it hurt to open my eyes and see where I was going. Carefully, I placed my feet on the cold hardwood floors, first my toes and then my heels. I felt the walls for the direction of the bathroom. I wasn't supposed to shower for a few days, but I desperately wanted to feel like myself again – fresh and in control of my own life.

I tried to open my eyes, but the fluorescent light, or any light, made me shut them immediately. For a brief, fuzzy moment, I could make out the dried blood on my face in the mirror. Twisting the shower on and stepping in, I didn't get my head wet, only the back of my scalp. My throat was scratchy from the intubation tube that had been down my throat. A girdle was Velcroed around my waist, and, due to the fat extraction, my hips were black and blue.

As I grabbed for a towel, I couldn't believe one little eye job was serious fucking surgery, *Well, four surgeries if you count the laser procedures.* I dressed and allowed the nurse to lead me to the car waiting for us in the parking lot. I'd already hiked from my house to the hospital. Doing so again with a bloody bandage over my puffy eyes would move me from an adventurous patient to one with a death wish.

It seemed I had gone through the worst of it. However, when I awoke on Wednesday, the pain was beating my skull and eyes like a teenager on their first drum set. I became keenly aware of the stitches inside of my eyelid, and I felt it every time I blinked. My trauma from the surgery – the anesthesia, the incisions inside my eye, I couldn't put in my contacts, put on my glasses, or look at any screens; I had to sleep sitting up in my bed with like forty pillows behind me – was painful...yet bearable.

I refused all painkillers – Percocet, Valium, all of it – no steroids either. The only prescription I took was antibiotics. I considered myself "sober," not in the traditional sense of the word. I just didn't want to put a bunch of chemicals in my body. That was the old me and purely recreational. I would now rather feel the pain than dope myself up and do more harm to my body and feel dependent on medicine.

For the next three days, I descended into a darkness that felt both physical and mental. I popped in my earbuds and absorbed episodes of different podcasts for four days. I relied on my other senses to cue me into the times of the day.

Sitting upright with my eyes bandaged transported me back to one particular moment: the dark room where I used to develop photos, 20 years ago. I could feel the cool water of the developer beneath my fingers, feel the rush of excitement as shapes and forms came up on the paper and became photographs I'd taken hours or days before. I lifted them out of the developer and used clothespins to attach them to a string that hung across the room. I watched them dry and wondered how they would look in their final form. *Had I captured the moment as I saw it? Had I made a statement for myself about the subject?*

The time warp of imagining myself transforming negatives into beautiful prints, hanging the wet photos on a clothesline to dry and come to life, became an image I replayed over and over again. As someone who lived for moments and lived within them and didn't consider the future, this was turning into a nightmare. My mind went to places it never goes.

What if I never saw again?

Or I never saw how I "used to?"

My whole existence was to tell stories through my eyes. I was faced with not being able to "look" back through it all because I had to heal and rest – to wonder if the best was behind me. Forced to look inward, with only podcasts for company and an occasional visit from my girlfriend and my house manager, I wondered, "Would my temporary, forced hiatus become a permanent one?" Life had already changed at the speed of a shutter.

My ability to see had never been unreliable in my life. Sounds could deceive me, thinking, for example, a car was actually just the wind, but sight, that was the one that got me paid to become the person everyone knew me as: the "celebrity photographer," the one who danced with the world's most famous people, the one who could make any image he wanted with the snap of his fingers and a "let's go go go." I moved and snaked around on the ground of every shoot, my eyes a merciless, all-seeing homing device. I was going to get the shot. I always did.

When Whoopi inducted me into the New Jersey Hall of Fame, she called me "one of the great eyes on the planet." This compliment not only touched me but resonated as a beautiful tribute to our friendship and my career. These eyes didn't have it right now. Even when I healed, I had to face a fearful reality that they may never have it again.

* * *

On Thursday, I had to get out – only to get into an even smaller, more cramped space. I took an Uber to hyperbaric therapy, where I slid into what amounted to an iron lung filled with pure oxygen. This was supposed to lead to a quicker healing time. The room had eight of these large glass tanning-bed-like devices, costing about a quarter of a million each. I took off my jewelry, and one of the attendants rolled me into one of the tubes. Big screen TVs screamed from within the clear chamber, which, of course, I couldn't look out of because my eyes still shied away from the dimmest of lighting. The futuristic device sent me into a space-like trance, until a voice came over on what sounded like a broken loudspeaker at a fast-food restaurant.

"HEY, TIM, YOU OK IN THERE?" a man's voice blared.

"I'm fine," I said quietly, wincing at the surprise and loudness of the sound.

"Ok, good, keep relaxing!"

My *Star-Trek*-like chamber may have been oxygenizing my body, but I yearned to see what was out the "window." However, it was too painful for me to look at my surroundings. Left to mentally fend for myself, I kept tumbling toward my darkest thoughts.

For perspective, the surgeries had been a success. The doctors found the detached retina early, and I was likely going to heal well. The elective surgery, too, seemed like it went perfectly, and despite the puffy face from swelling, I really felt good about it. But *hell*...it was all a reminder, a cruel knocking on the door, that I couldn't rely on my vision forever. It, too, was fallible, like the rest of my body. No amount of carefully curating a set, a person's appearance or a blending of the two, no huge dose of confidence would make up for any physicality lost or on the way out.

Back home in my perfunctory sitting position, I fumbled for my phone and called a client who had been leaving messages. I told them what was happening. Part of me wanted to cry, but I didn't know if that was allowed after an eye surgery. *Was that on the list of no-no's? Was I someone who cared about the rules now? Should I keep in this deep pang of vulnerability and uncertainty, as I'd done for so many years?*

"Tim, you'll be fine," my client said when I started talking about life and work. My staff was running my gallery without a single call or email to me. This should have been a good thing, but it made me wonder if they could do it all without me, in perpetuity. "This whole experience will be part of the story and your legacy."

When I was a younger photographer, I used to flippantly say, "When I die, my name doesn't need to be on it, but the work needs to carry forward." It was my way of acknowledging that the photos I was taking were historically important but admitting that, in the end, I didn't matter...my subjects did.

However, as soon as I said the words, I wondered, "Maybe I did want a legacy." It never used to be about thinking that I mattered. The work mattered. My words to my client were flippant, nihilistic. The truth is it did matter. You live, you work, and you create your legacy.

I used to say, "I'm just gonna die without notice; I'm just a guy behind the lens." But I know now that it meant something more. I had created not just my own legacy but the legacy of others. It became something that represented my time here on earth.

I spend my life creating this imagery that's history based. I documented pop culture in my time but got lost, in a sense, and full of myself because of my success and my upbringing. It all comes back around, though, and I downplayed that I was important, although, in my head, my ego knew better. My downplaying myself was all a defense mechanism, masking my insecurity and fear of appearing self-absorbed. As I put down the phone, I realized I *had* created a life and body of work I was proud of.

Saturday was the first time that the morning light didn't hurt my closed or semi-closed eyes. The bandages were on for the first two days. I then had to wear strips of surgical tape under my eyes, making me look like a football player or Native American warrior. I was no longer the hiking, unauthorized-shower-taking, hyperbaric-chamber, new-age person I was a mere five days ago. I hesitated before fully exposing myself to the sunlight, something I never did. However, there was no other way but to just go for it; I had to quell the fear of my eyesight not being perfect again. Perhaps, I would see in a different way, and that wasn't bad or "the end." Seeing was a result of mind and light playing together. You could "see" without your eyes, without people, without anything. My experience with a camera – and the anxious recovery process after the surgery – taught me that seeing comes from being present, the presence that told you what was good and what didn't work, the focus that knew you got the right shot or made a correction at just the right time. It was the little voice that said, "I got this, Mom." The eyes were merely the gateway to that inner sanctum.

One of my friends later asked me what it was like to open my eyes again. I didn't have an answer and still don't. What I do know is I awoke to a glorious scent and majestic view that reminded me I was loved and very much seen: a vase of fresh cherry blossoms.

Chapter 24
LA Story

Sometime around 1990, I was going back and forth so much to Los Angeles that I was becoming a fledgling member of the frequent flyer club. My travel agent at the time represented a lot of my celebrity subjects like Billy Joel and Bruce Springsteen and did all the travel arrangements for a lot of rock and roll tours. She put all of those people at *the* Rock and Roll Hotel in Los Angeles called the Sunset Marquis. She said that I should be staying there too.

I started to become a regular and was there quite often. It was really becoming a wonderful respite for me because it was like being on vacation. My clients flew me out of the cold New York winters to Los Angeles; all my expenses were paid; and I was put up in a hotel where I could lounge around the pool and enjoy the warmth and sunshine of Southern California during my days off.

It was a moment in my career when I was really taking off, and I was feeling great about myself. I was skinny and had long hair and looked very much like my rock and roll clients and was starting to live the same lifestyle. I was lounging around the pool at the Sunset Marquis one afternoon, wearing a Speedo, all greased up with the tanning lotion of the moment, Bain de Soleil, or some other concoction, which made me as dark as a Jersey kid would want to be during the summer months, even though it was the winter in Los Angeles.

One afternoon, I was lounging around the pool when the manager of the hotel, whom I had gotten to know quite well, came up to me.

"There's somebody who wants to meet you," he said. "Can I bring him up here, and would you mind if I introduced him to you?"

"Of course," I replied. "Bring him over."

That guy turned out to be a photographer by the name of Jim Marshall. Jim Marshall was probably the preeminent and best rock-and-roll photographer who ever lived. Jim was maybe 25 years older than me, but I was very aware of who he was and of his career. He was quite crusty from years of alcohol, drug abuse and being fully immersed in the rock-and-roll lifestyle.

When he came up to me, he introduced himself and said, "I'm a big fan of your work. I've been seeing your photos in *Rolling Stone*, and I just wanted to meet you."

He caught me so off guard that I just said, "Are you kidding me?! You're a legend."

Well, I was blown away because this was someone whose work I revered. This was somebody who really was the real deal. I never saw myself as a real photographer. I was just a smart aleck youngster from New Jersey who happened to get lucky enough to start to take pictures of famous people.

Well, we started talking and sharing stories. One thing led to another, and we ended up back in his room, showing me photographs, and then we went to the bar. He wanted to have one of my images. He had flipped over that picture of Robert Mitchum that I had done and really wanted a copy, and I wanted one that was so similar of Jim Morrison that he had done. It became this mutual, respectful, and loving friendship that lasted many,

many years. We met whenever he was in New York, and I met him whenever I was on the West Coast, in either Los Angeles or San Francisco, where he lived.

He was a really brash guy. I used to jokingly say he was the only hipster bigot, someone who was unapologetic in whatever came out of his mouth. He said anything and everything he wanted and to me was honest with himself. He was an alcohol and drug infused parody of what a journalist of his caliber represented, but he was also a really sweet man who had a huge heart and who would actually kill for you if he thought someone was jeopardizing your safety. He was a gun toting, odd-looking little man who had a distorted nose but a big heart. He was funny, brash and loving, and I loved him as much as he loved me.

There are so many stories around Jim. I'm not the only one who has them. Jim could put objects up his nose and pull them out the other side, given his destroyed septum from years of nasal abuse. I remember being in a restaurant once where he ordered a steak. When the waiter brought over a steak knife to go with his meal, he responded by pulling out a huge hunting knife and saying, "You call that a knife?" and showed the waiter his. He hated onions with a passion and would tell everyone, and if someone ordered them or brought them to him after he told them he didn't want onions, he would actually throw the plate at the waiter. He was known for throwing a plate of onions down the hallway of the Sunset Marquis Hotel, forcing the management to banish him for a period of time. On another occasion at the Marquis, he left his .357 Magnum under a pillow in his room after checking out. He forgot it was there, and a housekeeper freaked out after finding the weapon, again causing the management to ban his stay for a period of time.

Many similar stories at the Sunset Marquis preceded him, but Jim had this loving side to him that was infectious. He was a barfly and spent many hours there and built friendships and relationships with so many people who not only were curious and interested in his distinct personality, but were always blown away and impressed with the career and the level with which his iconic photography documented musicians and celebrity. We befriended each other for over 25 years and had a great relationship built on respect and admiration.

Jim had been involved in a gallery that had recently opened up called the Morrison Hotel Gallery. Henry Diltz, one of Jim's contemporaries who was another amazing music photographer in his own right and documented that scene throughout the sixties and seventies, was the staff photographer for Woodstock and the Monterey Pop Festival. He did hundreds of well-known album covers, including the first Crosby, Stills, and Nash cover, James Taylor's *Sweet Baby James*, and The Doors' *Morrison Hotel*.

Henry, together with a music executive from Capitol Records whom he'd worked with many times over the years by the name of Peter Blatchley, opened a pop-up gallery of Henry's work in the SoHo section of New York City, and it was very successful. Peter and Henry stood across the street one day, seeing the flow of people in and out of the gallery and decided they should make it a permanent business. They saw Henry's picture of The Doors' *Morrison Hotel* album image in the window and decided that it would be a great name for the gallery. It wouldn't have been practical to only have one photographer's work in the gallery, and they asked two of Henry's contemporaries and close friends, David Garr and Jim Marshall, to let the gallery represent their work as well. The gallery started to become successful, and as they began to consider other photographers, Jim recommended me, and I became one of the newer additions to the gallery, along with some of my other peers.

At one point, Jim and I were driving around Manhattan heading somewhere, but he had to make a stop at the Javits Convention Center to pick something up. There was a photo symposium going on there, and he needed to run in and see someone at the Leica Camera photo booth who had been sponsoring him. He asked if I would mind waiting a couple of minutes while he ran in. I think he had to get a portfolio or something that he had left with them.

"There's somebody here I want you to meet," he said, "an amazing photographer, John Botte."

Yes, *that* John Botte, the man who later became my friend, almost died on Gus's and my watch, and ended up marrying Elicia after she left me. However, at the time, he was someone interesting to get to know.

I guess John had been at the Leica Booth, and Jim brought him out to meet me. John had been a police officer in New York City for many years but was also a photographer and a respected Leica user and, like Jim, had a relationship with the company.

"I wanted you two to meet because this guy does amazing work, and you need to see it," Jim said to me about John.

As a note, this was just after 9/11. John, being a police officer and a photographer, had the opportunity and access to photograph the terror at the World Trade Center like no one else and became known for those photographs.

Jim and I had decided to work on a project together because we had recognized a similarity in our photographs. The more we looked at each other's work, we recognized a similarity in composition and subjects, only 25 to 30 years apart. We thought it was interesting that my picture of Robert Mitchum and his picture of Jim Morrison were almost identical in pose and how they were holding a cigarette and how they were staring at the camera. There were other very similar compositional elements in our photographs. As we started to talk about it and compare them over many drinks and partying over many nights in Los Angeles at the Marquis, we decided it would be a cool thing to put them together and to do a book and plan an exhibition.

Jim was a bit older than I was and did not take care of himself. We were very different people in that respect. Yes, I partied too, but I've always been a trim and athletic person who tries to balance my party with a healthful approach to life – Jim, not so much. Jim was kind of a mess and not really healthy around the time that we decided to do this book together. He needed help in getting the images edited and prepped as files to be printed in the book, and I had a staff in my studio in New York to prep the image files so that we could both present a unified presentation of the work for publication. We spent a lot of time together working on this project, and, of course, because of our friends and relationships with different people in photography and entertainment, our project started to generate a lot of interest. No two photographers had ever collaborated like this before, and unlike most photographers whose egos would not allow this kind of collaboration, we were genuinely excited about the concept and what we were doing together.

As the book came together and was ready for our publication date, we had organized exhibitions at galleries and an association with our mutual friend John Varvatos to exhibit the photos in all his clothing stores. We titled the book *Match Prints*, and on the cover was that one shot of Jim's and mine that started it all.

As the book unfolded, it was designed in a comparative way to show the unique and, oftentimes, whimsical and surprising relationship between two very distinct photographers. Jim came to New York as the book release was about to happen, and we were going to start to do our press. He was very sick. You could just tell he had flu-like symptoms and was coughing; he seemed run down and just not well in general. We were excited about the start of doing press and publicizing the book, but I was beginning to get worried that he wasn't up to it. The next day we were starting to do press and had an opening that night of our first exhibition at the Staley/Weiss Gallery in New York.

The morning of the first interview, we were supposed to go to CBS to be on Anthony Mason's show, *CBS Sunday Morning*, which was very exciting, given its visibility and the level of publicity it would bring to us and the book. I think our meeting was at 10 o'clock in the morning, and I started to call Jim to connect with him on how we were going to coordinate and get to the studio together. I was going to pick him up so we would end up walking in as a team. Well, I called, and I called, and was getting no answer. I figured maybe he was in the shower or maybe he was still having breakfast, but when I continued to get no response, I was starting to get concerned, given the way I had left him the night before. I finally got so nervous about our timing that I took a cab over to his hotel, which was 20 blocks away. When I got there and called his room and still didn't get an answer, I called security. I told them my worry, that I was very concerned for his health, and asked if they would come up with me and let me into his room.

Hotel security led me to his room, and after a few minutes of trying to get him to answer, we opened up his door and found Jim dead on his bed. He was curled up in a ball, wearing his Duane Allman t-shirt that he was wearing the night before when he was trying to convince John Varvatos he should sell them in his stores. This dear friend of mine, this rough character, was in a fetal position with an innocent look of peace on his face that I'll never forget. Later that day, we all met at my studio and had a meeting. *Should we continue? What should we do?* We decided that the right thing to do was to continue, to promote the book and to honor Jim by opening the exhibition; we decided we would do what was necessary to make his last project a success.

This was a very intimate and personal loss for me. Our friendship was great. I knew how he cared about me and about my wife and family, and he was always such a giving, yet brash and colorful, difficult man. He was also my brother, and I will always honor his memory. Jim was destined to be a legend because of the nature of his work. He was a brilliant photographer and took some of the greatest pictures of some of the most talented people in the history of the medium.

* * *

Back to the Morrison Hotel Gallery...I was a hustler. I still am to some degree. I was always excited about my career and the opportunities that were in front of me, and I had a recognition for my ability to create those opportunities. I became more and more involved in the gallery and became very friendly with the owners: Henry Diltz, Peter Blatchley, and Rich Horowitz. I became more involved in curation and bringing new ideas and people to the gallery, both as customers and as artists themselves, eventually bringing in Julian Lennon as a photographer we represented in the gallery, in addition to many others. I began to do other collaborations, as I had done with Jim. I did one with Barry Feinstein, another brilliant photographer and a contemporary of Jim and Henry's. Barry Feinstein had photographed a personality that really connected to a relationship I had with a similar-minded subject, and we ended up doing an exhibition together at the Morrison Hotel Gallery that was similar to the collaboration I had worked on with Jim. At some point because I became closer with the gallery owners and more involved in the gallery itself, the guys asked if I would be interested in being a part of the gallery and becoming a partner with them. It seemed to make sense, not just because I was a working photographer who sold my work and belonged in the gallery but because I was working with them to curate and to build the brand as much as possible. With my marketing and publicity experience, I thought that this gallery could be scaled and brought into a bigger marketplace and become a bigger brand.

When they asked me to be a partner, I really considered it despite my big life and career, and I thought about it as something I really wanted, though I wasn't sure how I would really fit or what I would do to bring enough to the table to make me an equal partner and to really make it something that both benefited the gallery and my already busy career. However, at that time, I started to have drastic changes in my life, as described earlier in this memoir, that forced me to consider a move to Los Angeles. The hotel that I stayed at, the Sunset Marquis, where I was so comfortable and so familiar with the owners, allowed me to stumble upon an idea. The idea was that this hotel, being the preeminent music hotel in Hollywood, that had this glorious history of crazy rock-and-roll antics and such an association with the music business, would be a perfect place to have a Morrison Hotel Gallery.

It was an *aha* moment that again, just clicked for me; it made total sense. As I was going through these intense changes in my life, debating a move from New York City to Los Angeles, I called a meeting with the owners of the hotel. We went out to lunch, and I presented an idea. They had a little gallery in their lobby, and I had a proposal for them.

"The gallery doesn't make sense," I said. "It doesn't really mesh with the pedigree of this hotel. However, I was associated with this gallery in New York, and I think you should let me take over the gallery you have in the lobby. Let us come in and put pictures from the gallery all around the hotel, basically decorating the hotel with some of the biggest names in photography and in music that would so represent the history associated with this hotel. It would give you such perfect decor, and it would provide us a way to build our brands together and make our brands connect to our clients and to the LA music industry."

We left that lunch shaking hands and agreeing, and the rest sort of became history. I moved to Los Angeles, worked with the hotel and the gallery and decided to commit because now I saw a reason for me to have an equal place in this gallery partnership. I was bringing something to the table. I actually moved into the hotel because I didn't have a home yet, which allowed me to put all of my focus on building out a new gallery space at the hotel. It was an exciting time and felt so good, especially given all of the issues that I had to deal with back in New York from my divorce and all of the other problems that I was facing. It gave me a way to stay in my industry. It gave me a way to continue to be involved in something new, to bring another business opportunity to myself, to do it in a new city with new opportunities and new friends with new enthusiasm. So I spent the time curating and building out the space, working to build on what we had just created, which was the perfect symbiotic collaboration. We decided to start to do publicity and activations with planned concerts and other things that would be thematically related to the curated exhibitions. We hired new salespeople, and I started to work closely with the marketing people at the hotel to do things that would draw attention and excitement to a place that already had the right to the photographs we exhibited.

As that relationship grew over the years, I continued to think about the end game. To me, the end game was to build the brand big enough to the point where we could expand it or possibly sell. My partners were older than I was, but I still had a ton of energy and another career in photography. The gallery needed to grow, though, and it was obviously scalable. The more I collaborated with the hotel, the more it worked for me and the gallery and became a big part of my identity.

The hotel had been around since 1963, but MHG brought a fresh injection of excitement and connection between it and the music world. It also expanded globally the presence of the gallery. It allowed us to promote and market ourselves around the world and on both coasts. The more involved I became, the more I started to meet people around the hotel, and I sensed that I actually became the face of it. The more people I met, the more we talked about the possibility of going further and expanding the brand. As we did that, I started to look for suitors, people who may have an interest to either invest in the expansion of the gallery or buy it outright from the partners.

Over the years, we managed to find enough interest, which gave us confidence in being able to sell it. It seemed clear that my partners also wanted to move on from the business, so we managed to find the right buyer. In doing so, we finally came to a place where we sold the gallery.

It was a moment of transition in my life that was very liberating; it felt like a success and the beginning of a new chapter.

Morrison Hotel Gallery had gotten me through a difficult period in my life, taught me so much, and expanded my identity in the industry. However, it was time to move on and to get back to what I do best. In 2023, we finally sold the company, and the four partners separated and went on our way. The new owners had decided that my abilities and involvement in the company were needed moving forward, and I stayed on as a consultant for a year and a half, doing the marketing and advising in everything related to my understanding of photography, the gallery business, and this company in particular.

The people who bought the brand had the potential to ruin it in my eyes because they were venture capitalists and were neither knowledgeable nor interested in a luxury retail business; they were certainly not creative people and did not understand the need for creative people to be recognized, accepted, and catered to. There are a lot of egos and personalities involved in photography, and the creative world is a different space. There was a soul to the Morrison Hotel Gallery that my partners had created even before my involvement, and together we grew it to a completely different level. My fear was that this new organization, this venture capital money, was not going to carry forth our vision for what we felt was a unique outlet for fine art, music and photography.

After a year and a half, it became clear that, despite my passion and input, my strong and sometimes difficult personality was not aligned with the future vision of the new owners. I was injecting a big part of my own personality and ideas into the business, and they decided it was time to move on from me. They wanted to make the brand more efficient and not be the definitive home for the niche we had created. In order to let me go, they had to navigate a contract with me that was involved and difficult to get out of, so they made up a cause to break the contract and get me out.

Despite all of my Jersey attitude and anger at the way it went down at the end, the impersonal nature of it and their disregard for my dedication to the company, I walked away rather than losing a fight with an entity that was much larger and had much deeper pockets than I had to fight. Although this was the right time for me to move on, given the forward movement in my life, it still hurt. It hurt because I was so passionate and put so much of myself into it; in some ways, it felt like yet another loss. It certainly was another betrayal. However, the lessons in my life were becoming clearer and clearer, and this was one of the most important chapters of my life. It too had left me with a scar, but once again I walked away stronger with another powerful lesson, grateful for the experience.

Chapter 25
A Moment of Liberation

One call had already changed my life.

And yet, another one would too.

A dear friend called and said they needed someone to photograph their home on the coast of Sardinia. After Sicily, Sardinia is the second-largest island in the Mediterranean Sea. It's one of the 20 regions in Italy located west of the Italian Peninsula and immediately south of the French island of Corsica. Apart from that little history lesson, it's drop-dead gorgeous with its clear blue ocean waters, friendly people, and an unmatched feeling of serenity. It's also what they call a blue zone, which means it's one of the healthiest places on the planet to live, and the population's longevity is proof. I'd visited before as a tourist; this would be my first time there on assignment, a la the good ol' days in South America.

I was game for the adventure. I looked into my schedule and travel arrangements, bought my ticket, and went.

While on the plane, I was finishing up the closing of a business deal on the ground. After over a decade of working with the Morrison Hotel Gallery and many months of due diligence, I finally sold our gallery to a venture capital firm. This was huge. Part of the deal was that I stay on as a consultant. My role would be as creative director. I was grateful for the sale, as it was going to afford me the ability to pay off debts that had followed me for years. It was also a milestone in my career; I was leaving behind something I'd built for a decade, and I was shifting into a more advisory role advancing my career in yet another area of photography. The change of pace felt exciting, yet there was a peace that I felt. I felt different then I'd ever felt before. Maybe it was the completion of a long focus on selling the gallery, or maybe it was about the changes that would likely occur in my life. Subconsciously, my mind was wondering what was next.

Once I landed in Sardinia, a car picked me up and took me on the hour and a half drive to this home. The scenery whizzed past my car window; the blue waters glistened, sparkling in my eyes. The verdant green, tree-covered mountains rolled by, topping the rock formations that hugged the white sand coastline. It was a beautiful, large beachfront property, with gardens all around the traditional Mediterranean stone structure. The staff greeted me warmly.

At sunrise, I started shooting photos around the house and property as the chef made breakfast. As someone who had stayed in the house before purely as a friend, and not doubling as a photographer, I felt at ease in the space. I started taking photos right away, day and night, walking around the house and property looking for interesting perspectives. In the morning, I'd shoot images at sunrise over the yard and the pool from the second floor. I saw fishing boats going out to sea and seagulls cawing. I didn't have to do much to make the scenery look beautiful.

I even shot pictures in the middle of the night. I'd go into the sleeping quarters in a separate wing, and I would do time exposures to be able to see the city lights reflecting on the water outside the windows. Then with a flashlight, I painted with light during the time exposures to make the room interesting with the scattered illumination. If I had turned on the room lights, then there would've been reflections in the glass and not have made the city lights so clear. And so I made it moody and gave it a different point of view. And I had fun late into the night, just by myself, drinking wine and playing with my photography.

After eating breakfast each morning and having taken photos, I walked into town which is just about a mile and half from the property. I wanted this friend to have unique photos, and in my typical fashion, I was drawn to the personalities of the town milling by, people in the small stores, a seaside town in motion. I would say hi to people, ask what they were doing, and take some snaps along the way. I couldn't help but include people in what was supposed to be a shoot of the house and the surrounding geographic area. It was all part of the feeling I was trying to get across.

It was July and a heat wave. By midday, sweat was pouring down my back. As I walked around town, I got so hot that I sought refuge at the shore. This was a fishing village, so there was water all around. I'd take off my shoes and shirt, hide my camera, beneath my shirt, and jump in the ocean with the other townspeople looking for relief. I was by myself and didn't speak the language, yet I enjoyed the time alone. On another day, I didn't even go to town, I just walked in another direction along the shore for hours. I didn't see a soul as I walked and would just stop in these little different beach coves and plop in the water and just sit there and think.

I began to realize that I was truly living in the moment, even more so than I ever had before. There was no big celebrity shoot to run off to, no business or employees to deal with– my only requirement was to take nice photos of a house. The gallery was not my responsibility anymore, and I felt the big change coming in my life. I felt the edges of what true inner peace could feel like. I silenced the voices in my head telling me to go, go, go.

Perhaps I was just really relaxed like never before. Each morning, I eased more and more into my new routine. I took photos, ate my breakfast, meditated on the beach, and walked in the sand. Of course, this was all amazing. I was being pampered, right? The chef made me fresh croissants every morning and fresh pasta and raviolis for lunch and dinner. The staff picked fruit from the pear trees and made marmalade for those croissants. My tea was ready as soon as my eyes fluttered open each morning. I was in heaven. For this moment at least, I didn't need anyone else around.

No, this went beyond semi-vacation-induced relaxation. I began taking walks around the peninsula where the house was located. Then, I'd leave its confines and walk all the way around for hours around the shoreline. Unless I was in town, I didn't see anyone – no cigarette butts, plastic, or sea trash of any kind. Just a pristine beach. The citizens of Sardinia pride themselves on their self-sufficiency and the beauty of their island. It's not treated in a way that we find most places in the world where you find the remnants of man and his waste...it's not there. It's so natural and beautiful, and most of the food is from the island itself. I just walked around and sat by myself.

From the moment I left LA, I was ready to let go of baggage I didn't even know I'd been carrying for so long. I finally had my debts paid and money in the bank. I didn't have a nerve-wracking, high stakes project in the works. No calls to make back to the United States to keep whatever I was running going. I went on this trip knowing something was going to change while I was away. That in itself is an exhilarating feeling.

Each time I went into town with my camera, I captured a still life. Little, beautiful storefronts, more sailboats going out to sea. Families buying their fish, a couple holding hands as they walked down the street. When I reviewed the photos I took after a long day, I was actually happy with them. It was refreshing to be on my own capturing these scenes and not worrying about the relationships in my own life. I could have brought any number of people with me on this trip, specifically one of the women I was dating. But I was relieved that I'd freed myself from the entanglements I'd usually find myself in trying to please others and not protecting my boundaries.

I hadn't yet found someone I truly wanted to spend my life with at this point. I always believed that I wanted...needed...a partner. Now, in this very comfortable situation, and I was alone, I was allowing myself to see an open future in front of me. I hadn't felt that way before. All of a sudden, I realized I could do this. I was ok with a different lifestyle. Maybe alone. Something more peaceful, centered, and focused on something different than the life I've been leading in Los Angeles.

I had been out of a serious relationship for the past year. I certainly have many friends. But I intentionally decided to not take anyone with me on what could have been a very romantic trip. It was sort of like I knew I had to conclude something before I left. Something didn't feel right, and I wanted to be alone. There was this feeling of, again, some release or some sort of freedom by being myself. There was this feeling of living life on my terms. Finally, because of all that made up my life, all of the debt, the relationships, the marriage, the breakups, all these things, the loss of my aged parents...all things I didn't feel like I could release or felt like an obligation or a burden of some sort, was released. I reflected on whether it was true, did I really get everything I wanted? Or, how could I start to feel this way now, when I had lived a life where I always did it by my own whim?

But I'd only done those things in the presence of others. And for their approval or the challenge of them saying I could or couldn't do it. This time, I was doing this for me. That was the revelation. I was experiencing myself like I never had before. I liked the fact that it felt honest. It felt pure. It felt like I was in the right place. I felt comfortable being me. There was a freedom behind it that I'd never had before. There was this acute sense of life and time and this moment I am living. I thought about my life, both where I've been, where I've come from, where I'm going, how little is left, and being in the moment more than I ever have been ever before.

While I sat on the beach, I thought of my parents. I thought of my oldest friend Dan, who passed away only a few months before. The proverbial "life is short" realization. I all of a sudden feel like I have the resources to finally feel true peace. I don't just mean financial. I was reaching next level clarity and understanding and being exactly where I needed to be at this moment in my life.

Something began to happen to me, beyond the usual vacation or work-from-paradise situation that had become a part of my career. A new rhythm began to emerge from within myself. Soon, my new routine transformed into a ritual: Walking into town and being with myself or just getting lost midday for hours, walking along the coastline, not seeing a fucking soul, just sitting in the water on the shore and cooling off and just meditating. I was so enjoying the alone time and so enjoying Sardinia even though I'd just been there three months prior. I was super comfortable and by myself, and I found myself saying, "Could I do this? Could I live here? Could I give up my old life?"

Yeah, I could do this.

I could leave it all behind in LA.

***

I began to explore the houses in the same area to see what, if any homes were affordable in this paradise. The house next door was empty and unique and really caught my eye. It was beautifully designed and was probably built in the 50's or 60's. Sort of Frank Lloyd Wright meets a Mediterranean style. I approached the owner who had inherited the house but only came a couple of weeks a year. I had this vision of me buying this cool home next door to my friend and us living out our old age in Sardinia together as neighbors.

My ask of her neighbor was turning into a campaign: I invited him to a pizza night at the house, which the staff was creating just for me so I could take photos of the scene. There was an outdoor pizza oven, and they spent all afternoon getting the oven hot. The neighbor came over and brought four friends. We drank wine and laughed. Meanwhile, I had an ulterior motive: I wanted to buy his house. My friend had already put the idea in the neighbor's ear; he knew I wanted to buy his home. It wasn't like I was obviously hitting him up. I just kept asking him questions: What was it like when you were a boy here? I schmoozed him and asked about his life. I learned his daughter was 17 and he was divorced. Perhaps he wouldn't want the house anymore. I was sitting there, like a spider, hoping to take over this web.

We said, "Arrivederci," to each other, for now. He'll sell it, eventually, I told myself.

After our dinner, I started texting my sisters, jokingly writing, *What do you think about moving back to the old country - Italy?!*

* * *

Before returning home, I took a short jaunt into the south of France to hang with my dear friend, Julian. It was so easy to just grab an hour flight to the south of France. It made me think of how great it would be to have a place in Sardinia and be able to move all over Europe with such ease. Julian took me on a long day trip to visit a friend in the mountains above Monaco. We drove all day through some of the most beautiful scenery and little villages. When we arrived in the village of Mons where his friend lived, it was a little paradise. I took pictures the whole way and was in the most beautiful place with one of my oldest and dearest friends. What I saw and felt just made me again feel like, what am I doing? I have freedom in my life. I don't have any children. I was a totally free man reaching a point in my life where now is the time to enjoy and to make a change and to do whatever. And would I want to live in Europe? Possibly. Wouldn't that be cool? How many people do you know who have that kind of freedom? Who can just say, I can go do this if I want. Nobody I know. Kids, work, family, money, mortgage...whatever it is...there's something holding everyone down. And here I am having this beautiful reflective trip, this moment, this opportunity to look at myself and back through my life and possibly make a decision for my future. I felt an energy that was freeing and made everything seem possible. This could be a very different way to live.

After ten days, I still had to return home, at least for now. As I began getting settled back into my house, I started to put my feelings into an even more realistic place. I wasn't tied to anything, and I thought what an amazing opportunity to realize my retirement dream in Italy. I had money saved up, I could get dual citizenship to Italy, which I'd looked into and always wanted to do anyway. A strong sense of relief washed over me; I could make this decision for myself, not in service to my career or my encumbrances.

We all travel and have that moment of, "God, I could live here." Why? Because you've left your life behind and you're not dealing with the everyday stuff that is your life. This was a different feeling though: Something had already changed my life, and that was the sale of my gallery. The feelings from this trip were confirmation that I was in a better place. It was this subtle passage of something that left me in such a peaceful state, and I'm trying to stay with it. Energy begets energy. It flows. Something's changed. Something's different. This was confirmation.

All of a sudden, things were very clear. I just felt really healthy and really light, aside from a bloated stomach from eating too much. I had cast aside some baggage.

I'm so grateful, I said to myself. *And I'm in.*

***

The next morning, I started looking up what I needed to do to become a dual citizen of Italy and the United States. I found a post on Facebook that explained it step by step. I texted my sisters again, who didn't take my last message of moving to Italy seriously. Now that I had a potential property, it was all becoming very real. I was a little surprised at myself: Really, did I want to live in a house with my sisters for the rest of my days? I must have been really changing a lot to want that to happen.

Sure, my sister Mary said. Not that I believed her.

But then what followed were all the reasons my sisters felt they needed to stay exactly where they were: Children, grandchildren. Things I didn't have to worry about.

Maybe I'd end up in the beautiful house on the beautiful island alone. Maybe I should take it in steps, I thought, spend six months out of the year there to start.

Could I do this? Could I live there? Could I give up my life, the money, the career?

The answer kept coming back: We'll see.

Right now, I'm still weighing where this life will take me, with all the changes and possibilities that keep coming my way. I found something on this past trip though, that I hadn't experienced before. A unique and visceral sense of peace that I think is the next part of my journey.

Chapter 26
Still in Motion

> *"It is important to expect nothing, to take every experience, including the negative ones, as merely steps on the path, and to proceed."*
>
> *– Ram Dass, from Be Here Now*

I've been a storyteller my whole life. For more than five decades, I've been behind the camera creating and telling other people's stories, and finally I'm stepping outside the frame and putting my own story in focus. During this season of my life, I've been lucky enough to reflect and take the time to look at these snapshots of my life and the moments I've created. I've given myself the ability to frame my life with a clear vision and a vulnerability that I hope in some way can give you the permission to be able to look at yourself more clearly as well.

I look over my life and ask myself, "What message do I want to leave behind?"

My life has been well lived, albeit with mistakes along the way, but bright and colorful for sure. I've had my losses; I've had my heart broken; I've had my disappointments. However, my images will remain to show others how it was, how it looked, how it felt, and that we were there. In some way that is the final truth I've been talking about, and that is what I'm leaving behind.

By writing this book, I've realized that it's not only healing to reflect on the moments I've had but necessary in order to keep moving forward. Friendships evolve, relationships may change, and endings can actually be a rebirth. I feel that by trusting in my strength, insights, and experiences, I have become closer to forgiveness, clarity, and peace.

Fifty years later...I'm still in motion. I don't know how I've done it all. I'm virtually sober. *Does wine count?* I know that I'm healthier in mind, body, and spirit than I've ever been. I'm still shooting, exhibiting, writing, producing....and I'm still setting cars on fire.

Epilogue
Reflections

My Birthday - Journal Entry
Monday, January 5, 7:00 a.m.

On the morning of my 70th birthday, I walked outside of our villa on the island of St. Martin. Around 7:00 a.m., with no one else in the house awake yet, I spend my time staring at an amazing cloud formation over the ocean. I want to wake my dear friend, Julian, as I know he loves to photograph clouds, but I also know he likes to sleep. As I look ahead, I see a rainbow in the middle of this thick, sculptural cluster of clouds. Although it's a sunny, clear morning with blue skies and white billowy clouds, there's a rainbow in front of me that I take as a gift from the universe to stop and recognize this special day.

As I stand staring out, drinking my tea, I start to count off the years of my life. As I count off the years, one by one, I try to associate an image, possibly an image of myself, whether I'm very young or at other different points in my life that I recognize and associate with that age.

I find it quite amazing that I can identify where I am in my life at each of those numbers that I slowly count off: from the people, to the places, to the accomplishments. It all makes sense. As I first start this trip down memory lane, I wonder if I'm going to actually maintain a memory for each year. Am I actually going to sit here and count off the years? But in fact, those years go very quickly as I count them off and associate them with the moments in my life that come to mind and make sense.

It feels funny, not only how quickly the thoughts and the counting go by, but it certainly seems to be a metaphor for how fast *life* goes by.

I'm going to take today to reflect as much as I can, as I have been reflecting so much lately in general. It's an interesting turning point in my life. I can feel the flux. I can feel something is about to happen. As I look back on this past year with such a heavy heart, all the emotional ups and downs and those that continue given this stage of my life, I know for a fact it is meant to be. Everything is meant to be for a reason.

I believe the gift of this new chapter in my life – that I am grateful for and that I look forward to – embodies that reason.

I walk a mile or so down to the beach by myself and come through a clearing to find the most iridescent, emerald green and turquoise blue water against a light, bright and beautiful blue sky. The clouds are way off in the distance as the early morning light keeps changing, and as with everything else, it's perfect. I take off my clothes and belongings and hide them in some bushes and begin to walk down the beach. I stop along the way and build a little stone sculpture, which I love doing, balancing and cantilevering rocks, and just think about the balance of life. The water temperature is absolutely perfect on my feet as the sun comes up and starts to feel so good against my skin.

I walk two miles down the deserted beach, picking up beautiful, perfect white seashells and enjoying my alone time, reflecting on my birthday and the water of the ocean breaking at my feet. As I get to the end of a stretch and walk back, I decide to go in the water for the first time. I stop at my clothes that I had left on the beach to check my phone and see if anyone is up at the house. There is a text from my friend Wayne that just says, *Happy birthday, Timothy. I hope you live forever.* It instantly makes me cry. Probably one of the most beautifully simple things anyone could say to someone on their birthday.

Then, I went in the water for the first time this year. I have been waiting for this moment for months. I just want to be in the warm water on my birthday and let it wash me clean at this moment in my life. I start crying as I come up with all this wonderful salt water all over my body and in my pores and ears and mouth and nose. I couldn't be in a better place at a better time, on a better day, with a better head space and a better mindset. And I couldn't feel more in love with myself, with life, with the people around me. I can honestly say on this day of days, in this new decade, I feel like the luckiest man alive.

I keep thinking of one word today and it's "journey." We all have our own unique version of that and understanding of it. In fact though, I wonder how many people really get the opportunity to think about it. To paraphrase a quote from my friend Julian's father, "Life is what happens while you're busy making other plans." A lot of us do not give ourselves the time to reflect, and I feel like I'm so lucky to be able to do so. Not only does it allow me to live my life with a certain consciousness and awareness, direction, and purpose, but also to be really specific in the way I live.

I also get to try and be as present as I possibly can. Most people have kids, bills and lives that prohibit them from being in the moment, so I don't take any of my reflection time for granted. I have this opportunity to look at life in a certain way. The time allows me to recognize I have something important to do. I know I've done something already in my life, and back then I didn't know what was ahead of me, but I have a good understanding of where my life is right now. I feel there's another chapter that's about to start and I'm about to accomplish something new.

As I walk home from the beach and after having this wonderful time alone, I get to celebrate my birthday with my friends. I'm so aware of all of my senses right now...my touch, my smell, my sight...I'm hearing the birds. Butterflies are flying around me. Beautifully colored flowers are everywhere in this wonderful Caribbean paradise. I couldn't think of a better place to be, both physically and mentally at this moment in my life. I have a feeling I'll be crying a bunch today and will need some moments to myself again. I'm also really grateful that I have my friends with me and that all these people have made such an effort to come and be with me on my day. It's unbelievably heartwarming and unbelievably gracious and generous of them to offer their time, effort, and, of course, the expense to travel and be here with me.

Someone could look at this scene in my life and confirm the answer to a question I asked myself a while ago: Yes, this guy *always* gets everything he wants.

But that would be too simple an explanation.

Do I *always* get everything I want?

No, not exactly.

As the Rolling Stones once sang, "...but if you try some time, you get what you need."

Love all around me.

Good friends.

A beautiful backdrop for a personal milestone.

Time for true self-reflection.

And more adventures to come?

I have to say this about the journey:

I'm not afraid.

I'm just not afraid.

Thank you

To Christina, for your faith, commitment, and dedication.
You make everything happen, even when I don't know how.

To Charles, for your trust in me.

To Francisca, for your eye, your insight, and your hard work.

To Whoopi, for the laughter, the trust, and for a lifelong friendship.

To Julian, for being the brother I never had.

To Joanne, without your perseverance and guidance this book would never have been completed

To Gus, for always being there.

To my sisters, Mary and Jamie; I love you.

And to Raquel, for sharing this journey with me.

ABOUT STORYTELLER PUBLISHING

At Storyteller Publishing, we believe stories are one of the last sacred spaces where people slow down, reconnect, and rediscover what matters most. Our mission is to champion voices with purpose, authors whose work inspires, challenges, heals, and invites readers to discover new worlds of imagination and truth.

Storyteller Publishing was founded by storytellers including bestselling authors, top publishers, and award-winning filmmakers who believe stories can change lives. We publish books that spark conversation, build bridges, and remind us that we are all connected by the human experience.

If our book found its way into your hands, we are honored. If it moved you in any way, even for a single sentence, we hope you will continue this journey with us.

Discover more books, authors, and upcoming releases at:
www.Storyteller.Media

For more on our films and television series:
www.Curiosity-Entertainment.com

For inquiries related to this author including media, speaking, or partnerships, contact us at: contact@Storyteller.Media

Join our community for new stories, merch drops from your favorite authors, special events, and behind-the-scenes updates:
Instagram: **@StorytellerPublishing**
TikTok: **@TheStorytellerStore**

Thank you for supporting our authors, our mission, and the stories that bring us all a little closer together.

Stories Live Here.